JAPA:

Passports

And

Promises

PAUL ADEBO

TRIBUTE

This book is a tribute to every soul who has embarked on the arduous, yet hopeful, path of 'Japa,' leaving behind the familiar embrace of their country for the often-unforgiving shores of Western civilisation. It is for those who carry the weight of expectation, the ache of separation, and the relentless pursuit of a future that, at times, feels as elusive as the London fog. May your sacrifices be honoured, your struggles understood, and your enduring spirit find solace in these pages. To all the families navigating the intricate dance of cultural assimilation, economic survival, and the preservation of love amidst the profound shifts that migration demands, this is your story, engraved in ink and seasoned with the bittersweet tears of diaspora. May you find echoes of your own experiences, recognition of your triumphs, and a comforting reminder that you are not alone in this grand, often chaotic, adventure.

To my mother, whose unwavering strength was the bedrock of our journey, and my late father, whose quiet resilience whispered promises of a brighter tomorrow.

ABOUT THE AUTHOR

Paul has experienced firsthand the profound complexities and exhilarating challenges of adapting to a new cultural landscape. His deeply personal journey from the vibrant streets of Lagos, Nigeria to the often reserved yet dynamic shores of the United Kingdom lies at the heart of this story.

His work explores themes of identity, belonging, resilience, and the enduring strength of family in the face of adversity.

He brings a nuanced understanding of both the professional and personal dimensions of immigrant life. This book represents the culmination of years of reflection, shared experiences, and a passionate commitment to illuminating the often-unseen realities of building a new life in a foreign land.

Paul holds a BSc (Hons) in Applied Physics, MBA from the University of Wales, and a Postgraduate Certificate in Business Research Methods from Edinburgh Business School in Scotland. He has worked in consulting, international development, banking, and now in the energy sector.

Paul is happily married to Gloria, and they live in Scotland with their two children.

ACKNOWLEDGEMENT

This story is woven from many threads, shaped by the lives, voices, and generosity of those around me. I am profoundly grateful to my family, whose steadfast love and belief have been my anchor through every season. To my wife, Gloria, thank you for being a true partner in every sense, and to my children, who fill my life with joy and make the journey of parenthood deeply rewarding.

To my parents, who first nurtured in me the values of resilience and aspiration, and to my siblings scattered across the world, thank you for sharing your experiences so openly and wholeheartedly. Your support and encouragement made this book possible.

I am equally thankful to friends—both longstanding and newly found—who entrusted me with their stories, insights, and journeys of adjustment and growth. Your lived experiences have given this narrative depth and authenticity. To my literary mentors, your thoughtful guidance and honest critique challenged me to stretch beyond my comfort zone. Your wisdom has been a gift.
And finally, to every immigrant who has dared to imagine a different future and ever dared to dream of a new beginning, this book is for you. Your courage, perseverance, and hope continue to inspire.

TABLE OF CONTENTS

GLOSSARY

This section includes a short list of essential vocabulary that may be unfamiliar to readers and a brief explanation of cultural tones that shape the characters' experiences.

'Japa': A Yoruba term referring to the act of emigration, particularly from Nigeria, often implying a quest for better opportunities or escape from adverse conditions. The term is explored in more detail, outlining its modern usage and the complex emotions it evokes

Chin Chin: A popular West African snack, typically a sweet, crunchy biscuit made from flour, sugar, and butter.

Jollof Rice: A West African rice dish cooked in a flavourful tomato-based sauce, a staple at many celebrations and a point of cultural pride.

Diaspora: People who have spread out from an original homeland to live in other parts of the world, maintaining cultural ties to their origin.

CHAPTER ONE
LAGOS MIRAGE

WHISPERS OF THE WEST

The air in Lagos felt thick and heavy, full of humidity and the steady hum of generators. Weak streetlights tried to push back the darkness, their orange glow revealing swirling dust and heat. From the veranda, the city's noise carried through the walls: car horns blaring, vendors calling out, and neighbours talking about their day. Inside the compound, there was a rare sense of calm, as the city buzzed outside. A single lamp lit the living room, its soft light making shadows dance across the walls. Amid Lagos's chaos, this small space offered them a moment of peace, a quiet respite from the city's constant movement.

Kayode stood in the doorway, quietly watching his two children as they slept. Their breathing was steady and peaceful, their faces calm, unaware of the significant changes ahead. He sighed deeply, feeling the weight of his hopes for something more—he thought of the United Kingdom. That name had called to him for a long time. It was more than a spot on a map; it was a dream, a far-off place full of promise. He imagined a country where opportunities were everywhere, where every child had the right to education, and where each street seemed to offer hope for a better life. In his mind, it was a place without the constant worries that filled his days in Lagos.

His wife, Amina, moved around the kitchen, cooking a late meal with practised ease. The sounds of pots and pans, and the gentle sizzle of oil, blended with the generator's steady hum. She hummed a quiet Yoruba song from her childhood. When their eyes met in the lamplight, he saw the same hope in her gaze. They shared a dream of a better future, and her steady support was the foundation of Kayode's plan. Watching her, he felt grateful for her strength and partnership. This journey, this 'Japa', was something they were doing together. Even in this moment of unity, he felt a quiet sadness for the life they were about to leave—the routines, the chaos, and the comfort of home. As they prepared for the next step, the air was filled with anticipation and silent goodbyes to everything familiar.

The idea of moving to the United Kingdom (UK) was always present in their home. It wasn't just about changing countries; it felt like a chance to change their whole way of life. In Lagos, ambition often felt like running in place—working hard but not moving forward. The UK seemed different, a place where hard work could pay off. People described it as a land where things worked, where opportunities were real, and where children could reach their full potential. The promise of better education was powerful. They pictured clean classrooms, caring teachers, and lessons that helped children grow and succeed. It wasn't just about good grades; it was about giving their kids the tools to face life's challenges and avoid the worries their parents had known.

He remembered many evenings spent poring over online brochures, university websites, and expat forums. The UK felt like more than just another country. It seemed like the answer to the problems they faced in Lagos. Daily life in Lagos meant power cuts, unreliable water, and traffic that turned short trips into long ones. The UK promised relief from these struggles. There, public transport worked, clean water was always available, and electricity was in constant supply. Kayode imagined a life where he could focus on helping his family grow, not just on keeping things running. While he dreamed of what could be, his wife took care of the details. She researched visa requirements, planned their finances, and ensured every Naira was saved. Her support was active and strong. When he felt overwhelmed, her calm voice reassured him. “We have to do this, Kayode,” she would say, touching his arm. “For the children. For their future.” Her belief in the ‘Japa’ dream was as strong as his, possibly even stronger, driven by her deep wish to protect their children from the hardships of home.

He remembered one evening, just weeks before they were set to leave. The Lagos air was thick, the humidity clinging to their skin. They sat together on the porch swing, gently swaying as distant music and the hum of the generator filled the background. Their two children, Maya and Kofi, were already asleep, their quiet breaths reassuring. Amina was unusually quiet, her gaze fixed on the sky. Then she turned to him, her eyes full of hope and a touch of longing. “Imagine it, Kayode,” she said softly. “No more worrying about school fees that keep rising. No more worrying about the children catching malaria at night. Just peace. And opportunity." She hummed a fragment of an old lullaby, a tune from their mothers, a melody that spoke of home and dreams. Her eyes showed shared sacrifices, commitment, and belief in the promise ahead. This was their shared dream, built on hope, anticipation, and a touch of sadness for the life they were about to leave behind.

The appeal of moving West, known as the 'Japa' phenomenon, was not just Kayode's personal dream—it was shared by many. It reflected a common hope for a safer, more advanced life. The UK was seen as more than a place to work or study; it represented a better way of living. People believed things worked there, systems were reliable, and the future felt more secure. Stories of success, often shared and sometimes exaggerated, made this dream even more tempting. The message was clear: leave Nigeria for the UK, and life would get better. Education would be excellent, healthcare would work, and there would be many opportunities. This was the dream that called to so many.

Kayode, like many of his peers, had internalised this narrative deeply. He saw the move not as an escape but as a profound act of responsibility, the ultimate expression of his role as a provider. To deny his children the opportunities the UK supposedly offered would be a failure of his paternal duty. It was a validation of his manhood, a testament to his ability to secure a better future for his lineage, a future unburdened by the systemic frustrations he himself had endured. This internalised pressure, this societal mandate for upward mobility, was a powerful engine driving the 'Japa' movement. It transformed the decision to migrate from a personal choice into an almost existential imperative. The whispers of the West were not just economic; they were social, cultural, and deeply personal, promising not just material improvement but a fundamental upgrade in quality of life. He felt the weight of these expectations, not as a burden but as a righteous calling. He was not just leaving Lagos; he was embarking on a sacred mission, a quest to bestow upon his children the gift of a life he believed was rightfully theirs.

He watched Amina humming as she moved from the kitchen to the bedroom, the scent of spices and simmering stew filling the air. Her movements were efficient, her focus on the task at hand, yet when her eyes met his, they held a quiet intensity. It was the intensity of shared purpose, of a dream that had taken root in both their hearts. She was sorting through clothes, packing away items that would not be making the journey, a tangible sign of their imminent departure. Her support was not just vocal; it was in these practical actions, these silent acknowledgements of the reality of their impending move. There were deep love and fierce protectiveness in her gaze, a silent promise to navigate this new world alongside him. Yet beneath the surface of her resolute optimism, Kayode sometimes detected a flicker of something else – a subtle shadow, a hint of unspoken anxieties. It was a familiar disguise, masking their individual fears behind a united front of unwavering determination.

This carefully constructed façade of unity, he knew, was essential. It was the bedrock upon which their hope was built, a testament to their shared belief in a future worth every sacrifice. He knew, with a certainty that settled deep in his bones, that this shared dream, this promise of a better life, was worth stepping into the unknown, even if the first steps were tinged with the sorrow of leaving behind all that was familiar. The air, thick with the scent of cooking and the distant symphony of Lagos, held the quiet dignity of anticipation, an unmistakable sense of an ending and a beginning of unity.

At eight, Maya's eyes held the restless curiosity of a hummingbird. They darted everywhere, absorbing the kaleidoscope of Lagos life. Her world was a symphony of sounds: the incessant chatter of her cousins, the distant call to prayer, the rhythmic pounding of yams in a neighbour's courtyard, and the ever-present, reassuring hum of the generators that seemed to power their very existence. Her younger brother, Kofi, who was four years old and a whirlwind of boundless energy, mirrored her passion for life. His days were a blur of watching Maya. At eight, she was always curious, her eyes taking in everything around her in Lagos. Her world was full of sounds: her cousins talking, the call to prayer, the pounding of yams in a neighbour's yard, and the steady hum of generators. Her younger brother, Kofi, was four and full of energy, sharing her excitement for life. He spent his days watching cartoons, building towers, and copying the adults' conversations, which always made their parents smile. He also had a magical white blanket that transformed the world into something entirely new. There would be parks, vast, green expanses where they could run and play until their lungs burned, unlike the dusty, crowded spaces they knew. And there would be castles, real, majestic castles, just like in the picture books, filled with knights and princesses and secrets waiting to be unearthed.

"And schools, my darlings," Amina would say, her eyes bright, "schools that are big and beautiful, made for learning. No more squeezing into small classrooms. You'll have everything you need to become the smartest children!" She described schools that worked well, where learning was enjoyable rather than a chore.

The idea of 'functional schools' was important in her stories. It meant a place where education was part of daily life, free from the problems and shortages they sometimes faced. It was a promise of order and a clear path to success, very different from the busy but lively life they knew in Lagos.

Kofi, with his limited grasp of abstract concepts, understood 'Japa' as a grand excursion, a prolonged holiday where new toys and exciting games awaited. The mention of castles and snow conjured images of a fantastical playground, a place where his imagination could run wild. He would giggle, picturing himself sliding down icy slopes or exploring hidden turrets. The idea of visiting 'shopping malls' – a concept he vaguely understood as places with an abundance of colourful things – further fuelled his excitement. It was a future where every day was a special occasion, a break from the familiar routine. He would ask his father, Kayode, "Dad, will there be a big, big slide in London? Like the one at the amusement park?" Kayode, caught between the weight of their reality and the necessity of his children's hope, would offer a reassuring smile, his heart a tangled knot of pride and creeping, cold dread.

Maya, however, was beginning to grasp at the edges of something more complex. While she was captivated by the tales of snow and castles, her sharp mind also registered the hushed conversations between her parents, the careful budgeting, the concerned frowns that sometimes creased their foreheads. She understood that 'Japa' was not just about fun; it was a serious undertaking. Her mother's explanations about 'opportunities' and 'future successes' resonated with her, even if she couldn't fully articulate their meaning. She saw the pride in her parents' eyes when they spoke of their plans, and she understood that this journey was important, a significant stepping stone for their family. Yet there was a subtle undertone to their narratives, a carefully omitted truth that Maya, with her developing intuition, was beginning to sense.

The contrast between their current life and the perfect version of London was a gap they were consciously trying to bridge with stories. In Lagos, their world was a vibrant tapestry of sensory overload. The aroma of suya grilling on open coals comes through the humid air, mingling with the exhaust fumes of danfos and the sweet scent of overripe mangoes. They navigated a maze of bustling markets, where friendly vendors called out greetings, their hands laden with everything from intricately woven baskets to shimmering fabrics. Their extended family was an integral part of their lives; aunts and uncles were frequent visitors, cousins were playmates, and grandparents offered a comforting, steady presence. The chaos was not a deterrent; it was the rhythm of their lives, a familiar melody that grounded them.

Amina often used analogies in her efforts to prepare them. "Imagine, Maya," she'd say, "that our house is like a small boat on a big, busy river. There are many other boats, and it can get a bit crowded and noisy. London is like a big, calm lake. There are still boats, but more space to swim and play, and the water is clean." She would tell them about the children in London who had their own rooms, who could walk to school safely, and who didn't have to worry about the generator breaking down. These explanations, while well-intentioned, further sanitised reality, removing any hint of struggle or challenge from the picture they painted.

Watching his children's excitement, Kayode felt a bit guilty. He knew the UK wasn't as perfect as Amina's stories made it out to be. He had read about homesickness, culture shock, and the challenges of adjusting to a new place. He knew that even good schools had their own problems, and that the parks could feel lonely for kids used to busy, social lives. The castles were just old buildings, not places to play every day. Still, he didn't want to take away their hope or make them worry about what might go wrong.

He remembered a conversation with a friend who had already moved his family. "They love it," his friend had said, a hint of weariness in his voice, "but it's not like the brochures, Kayode. The children miss the noise, the food, the familiarity. They miss their grandparents. And the snow, it's beautiful for a while, but it's also cold, and it makes everything difficult. They miss the sun." This was the truth Kayode was withholding, the truth he was trying to shield his children from, for now. He focused on the positive aspects, the tangible benefits that felt almost too good to be true from their Lagos vantage point. He spoke of the abundance of books, the access to technology, and the structured learning that would allow them to blossom. He emphasised the safety, the order, the predictability that was so often elusive in Lagos.

Maya, ever observant, once asked, "Mum, will there be other children who look like us in London?" It was a question that pierced Kayode's carefully constructed narrative. Amina, without missing a beat, replied, "Of course, darling. There are people from all over the world in London. And even if there aren't many who look exactly like us, everyone will be kind. And we will always have each other, won't we?" She pulled Maya into a warm embrace, her response designed to reassure, but Kayode felt the unspoken anxieties beneath her confident words. He knew that fitting in and finding a community would be a significant challenge, especially for children accustomed to the strong bonds of an extended family and a shared cultural identity.

Kofi, meanwhile, was busy demonstrating his imagined snow-sliding technique, his small body wriggling with delight. He imagined the snow would be soft and fluffy, perfect for making snow angels. He had no concept of the biting winds, the icy pavements, the sheer effort it took to navigate a landscape transformed by winter. His understanding of London was a vibrant, colourful caricature, devoid of the nuances of weather, social dynamics, and the often-monochromatic reality of long, dark winters. He saw the world through the lens of immediate gratification, his expectations shaped by a child's pure, unadulterated desire for fun and new experiences.

The difference was clear. In Lagos, they enjoyed a strong sense of community. Neighbours felt like family, always ready to help, share meals, and support each other. The calls of street vendors were a familiar background, showing the city's lively spirit. The heat, humidity, and noise weren't just annoyances—they were part of what made it home. Their childhood was filled with love, laughter, and the hope that came from facing challenges together.

Amina and Kayode were, in their own way, weaving a new tapestry for their children, one designed for a different climate, a different culture. They were meticulously selecting the threads, carefully choosing the colours, and deliberately omitting any shades that might hint at hardship or discomfort. They were building a dream, a mirage of a perfect life in a distant land, a dream that, while born of love and a profound desire for a better future, was also an elaborate shield, protecting their children from the complexities of the transition that lay ahead. Maya’s sharp eyes and Kofi’s boundless energy were set to embark on a journey that would test the very fabric of their understanding, a journey from the vibrant, chaotic embrace of Lagos to a world painted in descriptions they could only begin to imagine, a world that held both the promise of wonder and the inevitability of shock. The tales of London, so vivid and enchanting in their parents’ retelling, were a prelude to an education far more profound than any ‘functional school’ could offer – an education in the art of adaptation, resilience, and the often-painful process of discovering that the most vibrant dreams can cast the longest shadows.

A WIFE’S ACCORD

She stood by the open suitcase, a mountain of clothes and memories spilling onto the worn rug. Amina. Her name meant 'trustworthy,' and in her heart she held a deep reservoir of it, not just for her husband, Kayode, but for the future she was determined to build. Her hands were busy folding shirts and rolling trousers, her movements economical and precise. This was not just packing; it was an act of faith, a tangible expression of her commitment to their ‘Japa’ dream.

Kayode, she began, her voice a soft counterpoint to the rustle of fabric, “you must not worry so much.” She didn’t need to see his face to know the anxiety etched there. She felt it, a familiar tremble that had often accompanied him, a shadow born of the precariousness of their current lives, a stark contrast to the stability she craved. "This is the right thing for us. For Maya. For Kofi." She smoothed down a child's shirt, her fingers lingering for a moment on the embroidered initial. "They deserve more than… than what we had."

Her past was a landscape she rarely spoke of, a terrain marked by scarcity and the harsh realities she faced as a woman in her upbringing. She had seen mothers crushed by abusive marriages, their spirits eroded by constant struggle, their dreams reduced to the daily grind of survival. For many, marriage was the only perceived ladder out of destitution, a desperate bargain for security, often at the cost of dignity. Amina, however, had found Kayode, a man who truly saw her, whose quiet strength and unwavering love offered her a different vision of partnership. Their marriage was not an escape from hardship in the sense of seeking refuge, but a conscious choice to build a better life together, free from the shadows she had witnessed.

"Think of the schools, Kayode," she continued, her voice taking on a steely edge, though her expression remained gentle. "Imagine Maya in a classroom where the books are always there, where teachers are not worried about feeding their own families before they teach. Imagine Kofi not having to fight for space or strain his eyes in poor light. These children," she gestured towards their sleeping son, a small, peaceful form tucked under his mosquito net, "are so bright. They deserve the best life can offer. And the best, my love, is not here."

She walked over to the window, gazing out at the familiar, yet suddenly distant, Lagos skyline.

The hum of the generator, the distant blare of horns, the scent of charcoal smoke – it was the symphony of her life, a melody that had once felt so comforting but now echoed with limitations. "I know it is not easy," she admitted, turning back to face him, her eyes holding a depth of understanding that went beyond mere words. "I know the sacrifices. But we are strong. We have always been strong." She picked up a small, worn teddy bear, Maya's cherished toy, and tucked it carefully into the suitcase. "My own mother," she said, her voice dropping to a near whisper, "always told me that a woman's strength is measured by the burdens she can carry without breaking. She carried so much, Kayode. And I… I will not let our children carry those same burdens."

There was a quiet resolve in her tone that was more powerful than any grand pronouncement. Her own experiences, witnessing the quiet desperation of women around her, had forged within her an unshakeable determination to protect her family and give them opportunities denied to generations before. She had seen the toll that a lack of education and limited opportunities took, and how they perpetuated cycles of poverty and disempowerment. The UK, with its promise of structured learning and a stable environment, represented not just a better life but a chance for her children to break free from those cycles entirely.

"We will not be strangers in a strange land, Kayode," she assured him, her voice firm. "We will be pioneers. We will build something good. For our children, we will make sure they have every chance to fly. They will have the stability to dream, not just survive." She picked up a framed photograph of the four of them, their smiles bright and unburdened, and held it for a moment before carefully wrapping it in a soft cloth. "This is why we do this. For this," she tapped the frame gently, "and for what this can become."

Her optimism, while genuine, was also a meticulously crafted shield. Beneath the unwavering resolve, there were flickers of apprehension, moments when her gaze would drift and a subtle tightening around her mouth. She knew the challenges that lay ahead. She had heard the story. Her optimism was real, but it also protected her from worry. Despite her strong attitude, she sometimes felt nervous, and her expression showed it. She knew there would be challenges ahead. She had heard stories about discrimination and loneliness in a new country. She realised that the reality of 'Japa' would be much more complex than the perfect story she told the children. Still, she believed it was essential to stay positive and united. Showing her worries now would only bring doubt and weaken their hope. The task was to break down the overwhelming process into manageable steps. Each item sorted, each box packed, was a small victory, a tangible sign of progress. It was a way of imposing order on chaos, of asserting control over a situation inherently unpredictable.

"I have spoken to Iya Bola," she added. "She will help us find someone to buy the sofa. Mrs Adekunle wants the kitchen appliances. They are sad, of course, but they understand." She knew that leaving familiar faces and cherished possessions behind was part of the price, but she framed it as a natural progression, a necessary shedding of the old to make way for the new.

Her strength was not the loud, assertive kind but a quiet, enduring resilience, forged in the fires of necessity. She had learnt to be resourceful, to make do, and to find joy in small moments of respite. This journey, she believed, was the ultimate act of resourcefulness, a testament to their ability to adapt and thrive against all odds. She was not just a wife packing for a move; she was an architect of their future, laying the groundwork for a life that offered her children safety, opportunity, and a profound sense of belonging, a belonging she had yearned for in her own early life. She paused, holding a delicate Chinese teacup, a relic from her wedding. It was beautiful, fragile, and entirely impractical for their new life. She placed it carefully in a box marked 'Fragile – Send Later'.

"We will make the UK our home, Kayode," she said, her voice laced with quiet determination. "We will create our own warmth, our own traditions. And our children will grow up knowing that their parents dared to dream and dared to make that dream a reality." Her words were an anchor, a promise, a testament to the unwavering spirit that would see them through the uncharted waters ahead. The facade of unity, so carefully constructed, was not a deception but a strategic deployment of hope, a vital element in their shared journey towards an unknown horizon. She knew the challenges would come, that the gloss of the 'Japa' story would fade, but for now her resolve was clear: this was their path, and she would walk it with every ounce of her formidable strength.

THE PROMISE OF 'JAPA'

The word 'Japa'. It hung in the air, a whispered incantation, a potent promise that had become the lingua franca of aspiration across Nigeria. It wasn't merely a synonym for migration; it was a cultural epoch, a collective sigh of hopeful departure. To 'Japa' was to actively participate in a national narrative, a story woven from threads of disillusionment and threaded with the shimmering appeal of a life perceived to be lived in a higher register. It was the pursuit of progress, a desperate yearning for security that felt increasingly elusive on home soil, and an unwavering belief in the superior living standards painted by a thousand glossy brochures and amplified by the relentless hum of social media.

For Kayode, 'Japa' wasn't just a word; it was the culmination of every sleepless night, every calculated risk, every suppressed frustration. It was the ultimate act of love, the definitive proof of his worth as a husband and father. In the culture of things, the man was the architect of his family's fortune, the bulwark against the storm. Failure to provide, failure to elevate, was not just a personal failing; it was a societal condemnation. The pressure was immense, a constant, invisible weight pressing down on his chest, making each breath a conscious effort. He saw it in the eyes of his neighbours, in the hushed conversations at the local suya spot, and in the fervent prayers offered up in churches and mosques alike. Everyone was looking for an exit, a way to transcend the limitations that seemed to define their present.

The narrative surrounding 'Japa' was intoxicating, a potent brew of curated images and selective testimonies. Stories abounded of lives transformed, opportunities seized, and children blossoming in environments that nurtured rather than stifled. The ‘abroad’ was a land of plenty, where paved roads led to well-stocked supermarkets, public transport ran with uncanny punctuality, and attending school did not carry the looming threat of perpetual strikes or scarce resources. It was a land where electricity was a given, not a luxury to be rationed, where water flowed freely from taps, and where healthcare was not a privilege but a right. This idealised vision, amplified by the diaspora’s well-intentioned but often unvarnished accounts of their successes, created a powerful siren song, luring countless souls towards its shores.

Kayode had absorbed this narrative like a parched sponge. He had witnessed his father's sacrifices, the quiet dignity with which he had weathered hardship, and the limitations that had ultimately constrained his potential. His father, a man of immense character and integrity, had worked tirelessly, his hands roughened by honest labour, yet his dreams had remained tethered to the ground, never quite able to take flight. Kayode carried the weight of that unrealised potential, a legacy of unfulfilled promises he was determined not to pass on. He saw his children, Maya and Kofi, with their bright eyes and insatiable curiosity, as living embodiments of that potential, a spark that deserved to ignite into a blazing fire. To deny them the opportunity to flourish entirely would be a betrayal of his deepest responsibilities.

The decision to 'Japa' was therefore not merely personal; it was a communal imperative, a fulfilment of parental duty that would be judged by the sternest of arbiters: the future success of his children. Amina’s unwavering resolve and practical approach to the daunting task of relocation were a source of immense strength for him. She was the anchor to his sometimes-turbulent optimism, the steady hand that steered their ship through the choppy waters of their anxieties. While he wrestled with the emotional toll of leaving the familiar and the bittersweet ache of cutting ties with his homeland, Amina focused on the destination and the tangible benefits that awaited them. Her pragmatism was a balm, a reminder that this upheaval, as disruptive as it was, was a necessary crucible for forging a better future.

He often found himself lost in thought, replaying conversations and re-evaluating decisions, the sheer magnitude of the undertaking threatening to overwhelm him. The financial strain was immense, a constant worry. Every penny saved, every loan secured, felt like a gamble, a wager on an uncertain future. He would picture his children's faces, their innocent trust, and the weight of that trust would settle on him anew. He had to succeed not just for himself but for them. The narrative of 'Japa' had imbued him with a sense of purpose, transforming migration into a noble quest, a heroic undertaking. He was not just leaving Nigeria; he was embarking on a mission, a sacred duty to provide his offspring with a life unburdened by the limitations he had known.

However, the whispers of doubt were never entirely silenced. He would hear stories, often relayed with hushed reverence, of individuals who had ‘Japa’d’ only to find themselves adrift in a new land, their dreams shattered, their hopes dashed against the harsh realities of prejudice and economic hardship. He knew that the glossy brochures and curated social media feeds did not tell the whole story. There were sacrifices to be made, indignities to be endured, and a profound sense of displacement that could trouble the soul. Yet the prevailing narrative, the overwhelming tide of popular opinion, pushed him forward. To remain, to accept the status quo, felt like a failure of nerve, a surrender to circumstances he could overcome.

He remembered a conversation with his uncle, a man who had migrated to the UK decades earlier. His voice was tinged with a gloomy wisdom. "The grass is not always greener, my boy," he had said. "Sometimes, it is just a different shade of brown." Yet even those cautionary words were often drowned out by more compelling tales of triumph. The glamour of 'Japa' was too strong, the promise of a brighter future too compelling to ignore. It had become more than a desire; it was a necessity, an almost biological imperative for anyone who harboured ambitions beyond the confines of their present reality.

For Kayode, it was the ultimate validation, the tangible proof that he was a man who could provide, protect, and, against all odds, secure a better future for his children. It was the promise of 'Japa', and he, like so many others, was irrevocably caught in its powerful, hopeful, and often perilous current. He had internalised the societal message, the deep-seated belief that this exodus was the paramount expression of his paternal duty, the ultimate testament to his capability as a provider. The weight of this expectation, woven into the very fabric of his identity, propelled him forward, transforming migration into a deeply personal and profoundly public affirmation of his worth.

FAREWELLS AND FADED PHOTOGRAPHS

Murtala Muhammed International Airport, Lagos, was a place where people chased their dreams, yet left loved ones behind. Kayode stood among the busy travellers, holding Amina's hand tightly. Around them, everyone seemed to feel both hope and sadness. This was the reality of 'Japa'—the excitement of a new beginning mixed with the pain of leaving home.

His gaze swept across the faces of their assembled family. His mother, her eyes perpetually moist these days, clutched a worn rosary, her lips moving in silent, fervent prayer. She had cried for days leading up to this, her lamentations a constant echo in their home, a testament to the fierce, protective love she bore for her son. Beside her, his father stood stoically, his usual cheerful expression replaced by a gravity Kayode had rarely seen. The older man held Kayode's shoulder, his grip firm, a silent acknowledgement of the weight of responsibility his son now carried. "Go, my son," he'd said earlier, his voice raspy, "and make us proud. But do not forget where you come from. Let the lessons of this soil be your compass." A simple warning, yet laden with generations of wisdom, a reminder that roots, however deep, could still be nurtured from afar.

Amina's younger sister, Funmi, her face a mask of forced cheerfulness, dabbed at her eyes with a crumpled tissue. She had been Kayode's biggest cheerleader and most vocal advocate for pursuing this dream, and now her sorrow was genuine. She held onto Amina, their embrace a long, drawn-out affair, punctuated by whispered reassurances and stifled sobs. "Don't forget to call,

Ammi," she choked out, her voice muffled against Amina's shoulder. "And send us pictures. All of them."

Then there were the aunts and uncles, the cousins and neighbours, each offering their blessings, advice, and personal prophecies of success and warnings of potential pitfalls. "Watch out for the cold," warned Auntie Bose, her voice booming. "And the people. Not everyone welcomes strangers with open arms." Uncle Jimi, ever the pragmatist, pressed a folded wad of naira notes into Kayode's hand, a final, tangible contribution to their dwindling funds. "For emergencies, Kayode. And remember, the UK is not the paradise they paint it to be. Hard work is the only currency that truly matters there." Their words, a mix of hope and anxiety, spun around him, a testament to the collective investment their community had in their journey. Each embrace was a promise, each whispered word a prayer, each tear a testament to the depth of their love and the magnitude of their sacrifice.

Kayode's emotions were a tempest. The ache of leaving, the pain of separating from these familiar bonds, was a physical sensation, a tightening in his chest that made each breath a conscious effort. Yet beneath the sorrow, a fierce current of determination flowed. He thought of Maya and Kofi, their innocent faces plastered on the walls of his mind, their futures the very reason for this agonising departure. Their eager questions, their boundless enthusiasm for their new adventure, had been a constant source of strength, a reminder of the greater purpose that propelled them forward. He had promised them a better life, and that promise, that vow, outweighed the pain of the present.

In his worn leather bag, nestled among their essential documents and a few carefully chosen books, lay a small, unassuming photo album. Its cover was faded, the edges softened by years of handling, yet its pages held a tangible chronicle of their lives in Lagos. Here was Maya, a gap-toothed toddler, clutching a bright plastic ball. There was Kofi, a shy, solemn-faced boy, perched on his grandfather's knee. A blurry snapshot of a family picnic by the beach, the sun glinting off the water. A candid shot of Amina, laughing, her head thrown back, a moment of unadulterated joy captured for eternity. Each photograph was a memory, a fragment of their shared history, a silent witness to the life they were leaving behind.

He ran his gaze over the plastic-covered image of his parents' wedding day, a vibrant display of traditional attire and beaming smiles. This album was more than a collection of pictures; it was their anchor, their touchstone, a reminder of the love and belonging that awaited them, no matter how far they travelled. He intended to fill its subsequent pages with new memories of their experiences abroad. He would capture the first snowfall, the children's excited faces at a playground, and the quiet contentment of a shared meal in their new home. This album would be a testament to their resilience, a visual narrative of their journey from the Lagos mirage to a new reality, a story of love, sacrifice, and the enduring strength of family.

The announcement for their flight crackled over the loudspeaker, a jarring interruption to the emotional scene. It was time. The finality settled on Kayode like a heavy cloak. He looked at Amina, her eyes mirroring his own mingled emotions. They squeezed each other's hands; a silent promise passed between them. "We'll make them proud," he murmured, his voice thick. Amina nodded, a single tear tracing a path down her cheek, reflecting the harsh fluorescent lights of the terminal.

As they turned towards the departure gate, Kayode cast one last look back. The faces of their loved ones, a sea of familiar features stamped with love and concern, remained engraved on his mind. The air drummed with unspoken farewells, and prayers whispered on the wind. He clutched the photo album a little tighter. It was a physical embodiment of everything they were carrying with them – the love, the memories, the hope. It was a repository of their past and a silent promise for their future, a tangible piece of home to accompany them as they stepped across the threshold into the great, unknown expanse of the world beyond. Its weight was considerable, a reminder of the journey ahead and the precious cargo it carried. The photographs within, faded yet potent, were not just echoes of what was lost but indications of what was to come, a carefully preserved past ready to be woven into the fabric of their new existence.

CHAPTER TWO

FIRST STEPS ON FOGGY SOILS

HEATHROW'S COLD EMBRACE

The recycled air felt cool and thin, a stark contrast to Lagos's humid air. The passengers disembarked slowly, like a ceremonial procession. In the immigration queue, Kayode held Amina's hand tightly. The smell of anticipation and fear hung in the air. Maya and Kofi's faces showed awe and apprehension, their earlier exuberance now subdued. The scent of uncertainty mingled with the airport's musk. As they made their way through the terminal, the smell of adventure and new beginnings filled their senses.

Heathrow had always sounded like a promise, a place where new opportunities waited. But now, standing inside, it felt cold and impersonal. The airport was huge—high ceilings, endless shiny floors, and bright clinical lighting. The constant hum of voices in many languages made it feel nothing like the lively, familiar chaos of Murtala Muhammed International. Back home, goodbyes were loud and emotional, full of music and shared feelings. Here, everything seemed focused on efficiency, with little room for open emotion.

The children, usually so boisterous, were reticent. Maya, her bright eyes wide, clung to Amina's skirt, her gaze darting between the moving walkways and the unfamiliar signage. Kofi, ever the more reserved of the two, stood a little straighter, his small hands clenched at his sides, as if bracing himself against an invisible force. Kayode knelt beside them, forcing a weak smile. "Look at this place, my darlings," he said, his voice trying for a lightness he didn't feel. "It's like a giant city inside a building. So many people, so many lights!"

Maya, however, remained subdued. "Daddy," she whispered, her voice barely audible above the din, "it's… very quiet."
Kayode's smile faded. Quiet? It didn't seem quiet to him, but he knew what Maya meant. The noise here was steady and focused, not the lively, unpredictable sounds of Lagos. The bright colours and energy were gone. Everything looked muted—greys, blues, and many white uniforms. The air felt colder and less alive. It was efficient, but it lacked the warmth he remembered.

Kayode suddenly felt the weight of responsibility. He was supposed to guide his family and stay calm, even though he felt nervous inside. This was no longer the life they knew; it was the start of something completely new, where every step felt risky. He had promised them a better life full of chances. But looking around at Heathrow's size and order, he began to wonder whether he had misjudged how hard this would be, or whether he had made things sound easier than they really were.

The immigration officers worked quickly, their faces blank behind their screens. Each passport stamp felt like a small win, another step forward. Kayode noticed how efficient they were—no small talk, just the sound of stamps on paper. It made their entry feel official yet distant. He felt oddly detached, as if watching from outside. They were no longer just a family; now they were 'immigrants,' a word that felt both real and strangely impersonal.

Amina, sensing his unease, tightened her grip on his hand. Her eyes, though reflecting the same muted light as the terminal, held a steady warmth. "We're here, Kayode," she murmured, her voice a comforting balm. "Together." Her presence was a quiet reassurance, a reminder that they were a unit, a force to be reckoned with, even in this vast, disorienting space.

As they moved towards the baggage reclaim, the sheer volume of luggage waiting to be collected was another testament to Heathrow's scale. Suitcases of all shapes and sizes lay piled on the conveyor belts, a colourful jumble representing countless journeys and countless stories. Kayode spotted their two suitcases, their faded labels visible. He hoisted them onto a trolley, the familiar weight a comforting sensation.

The next hurdle was customs: another queue, another set of faces, a different set of questions. But here, the atmosphere was marginally more relaxed. The officers, while still professional, offered a flicker of human interaction, a brief nod, a polite enquiry. Kayode answered their questions clearly and concisely, his mind already racing ahead, trying to decipher the airport's complex layout, locate the exit, and find the familiar face of the contact person who was supposed to meet them.

It was Uncle Jimi's friend, Mr Adebayo, who had promised to meet them. Kayode clutched the piece of paper with the phone number and a hastily scribbled description. The anxiety of not finding him was a knot in his stomach. What if he wasn't here? What if they were left to navigate London's transport system, a daunting prospect even for seasoned travellers, with two tired children and a mountain of luggage?

As they finally cleared customs and emerged into the main hall, the space opened up, vast and echoing, filled with a sea of faces, each a stranger. The noise level rose as a mix of voices, announcements, rolling suitcases, and hurried footsteps filled the air. Information boards flickered with flight details, departure times, and gate numbers, an indecipherable language of transit. The children's eyes widened further, their initial apprehension now tinged with bewilderment.

Kayode's eyes darted across the crowd, his heart beating faster. He held the paper tightly, scanning the faces holding signs. There were names, logos, and finally a hastily written 'Ade'. And next to it, a man of medium height, with a kind face and a sense of urgency.
"Mr. Adebayo?" Kayode called out, his voice carrying a note of hopeful desperation.

The man's head snapped up. A broad smile spread across his face as he approached them. "Kayode! Welcome, welcome!" he exclaimed, his voice warm and welcoming, a stark contrast to the impersonal efficiency they had encountered so far. He shook Kayode's hand with genuine enthusiasm, then turned to Amina, his smile softening. "And this must be Amina. You have grown so beautiful." He then bent to greet Maya and Kofi, his voice softening. "And you two must be the little ones. Welcome to London!"

The children, initially shy, responded with tentative smiles. The immediate warmth and genuine welcome from Mr Adebayo began to thaw the ice of their apprehension. Kayode felt a significant portion of his anxiety drain away, replaced by a surge of gratitude. This was it, then. They had made it. They were on solid ground, and they had a friendly face to guide them.

Mr Adebayo helped them with their luggage, his strong arms making light work of the trolley. "Don't worry about a thing," he assured them. "I've got it all under control. Your accommodation is all set, and I'll take you there directly. Just relax and let London work its magic."

As they walked towards the car park, Kayode stole another glance back at the vast expanse of Heathrow. The initial shock was beginning to wear off, replaced by a dawning realisation of the sheer magnitude of their undertaking. The stark contrast between Lagos and this organised, almost clinical environment was profound. The air, as Auntie Bose had warned, was indeed colder. It was a chill that seeped not just into the skin but into the very bones, a subtle reminder that they were in a different climate, a different world. The light, too, seemed different, less direct, more diffused, as if filtered through layers of atmospheric gauze.

He looked at his children, their small hands now holding his and Amina's with renewed confidence. Their initial fear began to fade, replaced by a nascent curiosity. This was the beginning of their story, one he was determined to write with courage, resilience, and an unwavering commitment to the promise he had made. Heathrow, with its cold embrace and overwhelming scale, was just the first chapter in a much larger narrative. The fog might be thick, the shores unfamiliar, but they were here, together. And that, he reminded himself, was a powerful beginning.

The weight of the photo album in his shoulder bag felt heavier now, not just with memories of home but with anticipation of the new memories they were about to create. He knew, with a certainty that settled deep within him, that this was just the first step on a long and complex journey, a journey he was ready to embark on with his family by his side. The enormity of it all was tangible, a presence in the cold London air, but so too was the quiet strength of their shared resolve.

NAVIGATING THE WEB

The descent into the London Underground plunged Kayode into a subterranean world, a stark contrast to the airy expanse of Heathrow. The air thickened, carrying a damp, metallic scent that spoke of age and constant motion. Kayode, his hand still instinctively finding Amina's, felt a familiar surge of responsibility. The children, their initial curiosity aroused by the novelty of the escalators, now looked a little overwhelmed by the sheer crowd. Loud sounds assaulted their senses: the rhythms of trains approaching and departing, the jumbled drone of announcements, and the hurried footsteps of a thousand strangers, each seemingly propelled by an unseen urgency.

"Alright, children," Kayode announced, his voice a little louder than intended, trying to project an assurance he didn't entirely feel. "We need to get our Oyster cards. Mr Adebayo explained it, remember? It's like a special pass for the trains." He held up the plastic card Mr Adebayo had given them, a simple, unassuming rectangle that held the key to their immediate mobility. The concept of a prepaid travel card, so commonplace among Londoners, was new to them. In Lagos, journeys were often as simple as flagging down a danfo bus or negotiating with a taxi driver. This methodical, prepaid system felt a world away.

Navigating the ticket machines proved an unexpected challenge. The touchscreens offered a dizzying array of options. Kayode, used to the straightforward, cash-based Automated Teller Machine (ATM), squinted at the small print, his mind racing to recall Mr Adebayo's hurried instructions. "Top up," he murmured to himself, tracing the words with his finger. "Zone one, two…" He glanced at Amina, who was diligently keeping an eye on Maya and Kofi, mesmerised by the flashing lights and electronic displays. "This is… efficient," he said, a dry note in his voice. "But perhaps a little too much information at once."

Finally, after a successful transaction, Kayode distributed the Oyster cards. "Hold onto these," he instructed, his voice firm. "Don't lose them. We'll need them for every journey." As they approached the barriers, the children watched, wide-eyed, as people swiped their cards, the gates gliding open with a soft beep. Kofi, ever hesitant, paused, unsure. Kayode gently guided his hand. "Just tap it here, Kofi. See? Like this." The gate whooshed open, and a collective sigh of relief escaped them. They were in. They had successfully entered the Underground's web.

The platform was a study in organised chaos. People stood in neat lines, patiently waiting for the train. The air was cooler here, a welcome respite from the muggy warmth that had clung to them since their arrival. When the train doors hissed open, Kayode ushered his family aboard and found a couple of seats by the doors. The interior of the carriage was a symphony of muted colours and polished surfaces. Advertisements plastered the walls, depicting everything from holiday destinations to dental implants, a visual onslaught that was both fascinating and overwhelming.

“Look at the map, children,” Kayode said, pointing to the famously complex Tube map on the carriage wall. It was a dazzling, multicoloured spider’s web, representing the vast network of lines crisscrossing the city. “See? Each colour is a different line. We need to follow the Northern Line to get where we need to be.” Maya, her initial apprehension fading, leaned closer, her finger tracing the red line. “It looks like a rainbow, Daddy!” she exclaimed, her voice filled with renewed wonder.

The journey itself was an exercise in physical interpretation. The sway of the carriage, the constant rumble, the fleeting glimpses of station names flashing past – it was a constant barrage of new information. And then there were the voices. The distinctive British accents, so varied and often rapid, proved a significant hurdle. Kayode found himself straining to understand the announcements, often relying on the visual cues of the station names displayed on the electronic boards. He became an expert at lip-reading, catching snippets of conversation and piecing together fragments of meaning.

He saw the same struggle reflected in the faces of others around him, the newly arrived and the tourists, their brows lined with concentration. It was a shared experience, a silent acknowledgement of the linguistic and cultural divide that separated them from the everyday ease of the locals. He found himself constantly whispering explanations to Amina, pointing out things he himself was still trying to comprehend. "See how everyone stands on the right on the escalators?" he'd murmur, or, "They queue for the buses. It's not like back home, where you just sort of gather around."

Amina, ever more adaptable, absorbed it all with quiet resilience. She had a knack for observation, her keen eyes picking up subtle social cues that Kayode, caught in the whirlwind of practicalities, sometimes missed. She'd gently nudge him or offer a quiet correction, her presence a grounding force. "Kayode," she'd say softly after he'd almost bumped into someone, "they keep their distance here. Personal space." He'd nod, feeling a familiar flush of embarrassment, a reminder of how much he still had to learn.

The big promises that brought them here—job security, better schools, cleaner streets—seemed distant as they tried to settle in. The reality was tougher and less exciting than they had hoped. Even finding their temporary flat, arranged by Uncle Jimi, proved hard. The postcode was just a jumble of letters and numbers, and every street looked the same.

The British accent, which had seemed so sophisticated on television, proved a formidable obstacle in real-life interactions. The clipped tones, varied pronunciations, and rapid-fire delivery –

it was like trying to decipher a code. When Kayode tried to ask for directions, he often met a polite but uncomprehending stare, followed by a barrage of words that flew over his head. He learned to rely on gestures, pointing, and the universal language of a confused expression.

The next afternoon, while trying to find a local grocery store, Kayode approached a woman walking her dog. “Excuse me,” he began, his voice carefully enunciated. “Could you… show me… the food shop?” The woman, after a moment of polite confusion, replied with a string of words peppered with phrases like “just down the road” and “past the roundabout.” Kayode nodded enthusiastically, pretending to understand, and walked off in a vague direction, only to find himself eventually in a park, miles from any sign of sustenance. He had to retrace his steps, feeling a profound sense of inadequacy, until Amina, with her innate sense of direction and a more patient approach, managed to find the bustling supermarket.

The city's sheer indifference was also a palpable force. In Lagos, even in the most crowded markets, there was a certain warmth and a shared humanity that permeated every transaction. Here, people moved with a focused purpose, their eyes often fixed on their phones or on some unseen destination. A simple smile to a stranger on the street often went unanswered, met with a blank gaze or a polite, but distant, nod. Kayode missed the easy camaraderie, the spontaneous conversations, and the feeling of belonging to a community, however chaotic.

He realised that navigating the UK was not just about understanding the physical landscape or the monetary system; it was about deciphering a complex web of social norms and unspoken rules. He found himself constantly second-guessing his actions. Was he standing too close to someone? Was he speaking too loudly? Was his eagerness to be helpful perceived as intrusive? He observed the locals, trying to mimic their demeanour, subtle gestures, and measured interactions, but it felt like trying to replicate a dance he had only ever seen from afar.

The children, too, were adjusting, but their innocent directness was sometimes amusing and at other times awkward. Maya, with her boundless energy and inquisitive nature, would ask strangers direct questions that often left them flustered. "Why are you walking so fast?" "Where are you going?" "Why do you look so sad?" Kayode would quickly intervene, offering apologies and explanations, trying to shield her from any perceived rudeness. He understood her curiosity and her unfiltered perception of the world, but he also knew they needed to learn the unwritten rules of this new society.

Kofi, quieter and more observant, was better at blending in. He'd watch his sister's interactions with a small, knowing smile, then mimic her more subdued approach. He was a sponge, absorbing the new sights and sounds, and Kayode took comfort in his child's quiet assimilation, a sign that perhaps they would find their footing after all.

Even simple things felt exhausting. Every conversation, trip, and decision took effort. Kayode began to look forward to quiet evenings in their small flat, where they could finally relax. He and

Amina would talk through the day's problems, and sometimes their laughter made things feel a little easier.

"It's like learning to walk again," Kayode confessed one evening, stirring his tea. "Every step is uncertain. We're constantly on the brink of making a mistake."

Amina placed a hand on his arm. "But we are walking, Kayode. And we are walking together. That is what matters." She looked out of the window at the darkening sky, the distant glow of London a reminder of the vastness they were still trying to grasp. "It is a different language, a different rhythm. But we will learn it. We must."

He knew she was right. The shock was fading, replaced by a clearer understanding. The perfect image they had of the UK was gone, replaced by a tougher, more complex reality. Still, there was a chance to build something lasting. The confusion was real, but small wins—such as using the Tube, understanding a cashier, or finding their flat—were bright spots. They were no longer just visitors; they were starting to belong, even if it felt uncertain. Their journey had begun not with big moments but with the quiet sound of a London train and a family learning to find their way.

THE CHILDREN'S LONDON

Outside the train window, Maya and Kofi saw grey buildings and wet streets. It was a new kind of magic for them. The bright colours of Lagos were gone, replaced by shades of grey and a perpetually cloudy sky. Still, there were moments of wonder. The famous red double-decker buses, just like the ones they had seen online, stood out against the grey. Maya would press her nose to the window, point at a bus, and whisper, “Look, Kofi! It’s so tall!” Kofi, quieter, would nod, just as fascinated.

And then there were the black cabs, their classic shapes a familiar sight even in photographs. They darted through the streets with surprising agility, their polished exteriors gleaming even under the persistent drizzle. To the children, they signified understated, sophisticated power, a stark contrast to the often boisterous, colourful taxis of their former home. Kayode had tried to explain the system, the metered fares and the drivers’ seemingly encyclopaedic knowledge of the city’s streets, but the children’s imaginations had seized on the visual. They were symbols of London, tangible proof that they had indeed arrived in this legendary land.

But the persistent dampness was a constant, almost tangible presence. The fine mist that often settled over the city, clinging to hair and clothes, was a far cry from the intense, life-giving heat of the Nigerian sun. They missed the way the sunlight used to bake the earth and make the colours of their world sing. Here, even on what passed for a sunny day, there was a coolness, a subtle chill that seeped into their bones. Kofi, who had always loved to play outdoors for hours on end, now found himself retreating indoors after only a short while, his cheeks chilled and his spirit somewhat dampened. Maya, usually a whirlwind of energy, had been subdued by the chill.

Their new school, a modern glass-and-steel building that stood in stark contrast to the more organic, perhaps more colourful buildings they had seen in Lagos, presented a whole new set of challenges. It was undeniably impressive, filled with the latest technology and sleek, functional furniture. But it also felt... impersonal. The classrooms, though bright and well-equipped, lacked the familiar warmth and the slight disarray that spoke of lived-in spaces and boisterous children. The walls were adorned with neat charts and learning objectives, but there were fewer of the colourful, child-made artworks that had filled the walls of their previous school back home.

The playground was a dazzling landscape. Back in Lagos, playtime had been an explosion of uninhibited joy, an organised chaos of running, shouting, and spontaneous games. Children from different backgrounds mingled freely, their shared exuberance creating an immediate sense of friendship. Here, the social dynamics seemed infinitely more complex, governed by unspoken rules that eluded the children's understanding. They found themselves standing on the periphery, their exuberance met with polite, sometimes curious, but often reserved British politeness.

Maya, accustomed to her direct approach to friendship, would often walk up to a group of children, her face beaming, and ask, "Can I play with you?" The responses were varied. Some offered a shy smile and a hesitant nod, while others looked away, their attention returning to their established games. There were no immediate invitations to join, no easy way to join. It was a subtle dance of social cues, a subtlety that the children, with their Lagosian openness, found difficult to navigate. They were used to the immediate warmth and easy acceptance. This polite distance felt like a gentle rejection, a quiet but effective barrier.

Kofi, watching his sister's attempts with a keen, analytical eye, was even more hesitant. He observed the existing friendships, the subtle nods and shared glances that seemed to bind the other children together. He longed to be part of it, but the thought of approaching them, of disrupting their established order, felt daunting. He saw the same muted colours in the children's clothing and the same reserved demeanour that seemed to pervade the school. It was as if the grey skies had seeped into their very beings, softening their edges and muting their voices.

The playground games themselves were different, too. The boisterous tag and elaborate group games of Lagos were replaced by more structured activities or smaller, self-contained interactions. The children seemed to have their own intricate systems of alliances and hierarchies, as well as inside jokes and shared histories. When Maya tried to initiate a game of "pass the parcel," a staple of her former school days, she was met with blank stares. The idea of taking turns and waiting for one's designated moment seemed less appealing than the immediate, unscripted fun they were used to.

One particularly disheartening afternoon, Maya, having finally mustered the courage to approach a group of girls playing a game of intricate hand gestures and whispered rhymes, was met with a polite but firm "We're doing our own thing." Her face fell. She retreated to a bench, her shoulders slumping, the vibrant colours of her favourite dress suddenly feeling out of place against the dull grey of the schoolyard. Kofi, seeing his sister's dejection, came to sit beside her. He offered her a small, smooth pebble he had found, a silent gesture of comfort, but the sadness in her eyes reflected the larger challenge they faced.

The weather, of course, played a significant role in their diminished spirits. Back in Lagos, even a sudden downpour was often followed by a burst of glorious sunshine, a chance to run out and splash in puddles that would quickly evaporate. Here, the drizzle seemed endless, a persistent dampness that discouraged outdoor play. The grass was often sodden, the playground equipment slick and cold. The children missed the warm earth beneath their feet and the sheer joy of the sun on their skin. Their playfulness, so intrinsically linked to the warmth and light of their homeland, felt stifled.

Kayode and Amina watched their children's struggles with a growing ache in their hearts. They tried to encourage them, to remind them of the opportunities ahead and the reason they had embarked on this immense journey. But they also understood the profound, intuitive impact of their new environment. The children were not just adapting to a new school or social dynamics; they were adapting to a new climate, a new pace of life, a new way of being.

The vibrant, sun-kissed exuberance of their Lagosian childhood was being tested, its colours muted by the persistent grey skies and the quiet reserve of their new surroundings. The children's London was a world of iconic sights and sounds, but for now it was also a world of subtle exclusions and persistent dampness, a world they were still learning to navigate, one tentative step at a time. The vibrant colours of their past were a cherished memory, while the present was a canvas waiting to be filled with new colours, new experiences, and the slow, steady growth of belonging.

SHIFTING GAZE

The initial shimmer of fascination with London was beginning to dull, a subtle but undeniable shift in Amina's gaze. The carefully constructed narrative of a life of ease, a land of endless opportunity where worries would dissolve like sugar in tea, was starting to fray at the edges. While Kayode, her husband, remained steadfastly focused on the grand architecture of their future – the secure job, the burgeoning savings account, the promise of a better education for Maya and Kofi. Amina found her attention increasingly snagged by the immediate, the inconvenient, the persistently irritating realities of their new existence. The very things that had once seemed like charming eccentricities of this foreign land were now turning into irritations, like small pebbles in her shoe that refused to be dislodged.

The weather was the most challenging part for her. The dampness, which once seemed gentle, now felt like a constant chill she couldn't escape. Her colourful Nigerian clothes, so bright at home, now looked dull in the grey light. She often stared out the window, feeling tired and impatient rather than curious. The grey sky matched her mood, reflecting a growing sense of dissatisfaction she found hard to explain. She missed the intense, warm sun of home, which set the pace of their days and made her feel alive. Here, life felt slow, always waiting for sunshine that rarely came.

And the cost of it all. Every transaction, every purchase, felt like a minor battle. The price of a loaf of bread, a carton of milk, a child's simple pair of shoes – these were not just figures on a receipt; they were constant reminders of the gulf between the life they had envisioned and the one they were now meticulously piecing together.

Kayode's meticulous budgeting, his earnest explanations of utility bills and council tax, were logical and necessary, but they did little to soothe the gnawing anxiety that settled in Amina's stomach. Back home, there had been a fluidity, a certain improvisation that came with managing household finances. Here, everything felt so rigid, so predetermined. The ease she had so confidently anticipated proved an illusion, replaced by a constant, subtle pressure, a need to economise that felt like a perpetual state of scarcity.

The absence of her familiar support network grew more pronounced with each passing day. In Lagos, life had been like a textile woven from shared experiences and readily offered help. A quick call to her mother, a sister, a trusted neighbour, and a problem, however significant, would often begin to unravel, flattened by a collective effort. Here, she was adrift. The polite smiles of neighbours and the cheerful but ultimately distant interactions with shopkeepers were no substitute for the deep, ingrained bonds of family and community. She missed the effortless understanding and the unspoken empathy that had always been part of her life.

The small kindnesses offered by Kayode's colleagues were appreciated, but they were like drops of water in a vast ocean of loneliness. She found herself replaying conversations with friends and family back home, their laughter and familiar voices a bittersweet echo in the quiet of their London flat.

Amina's initial steadfastness, her unwavering belief in Kayode's vision, began to show hairline fractures. She was still the anchor, still the one ensuring Maya and Kofi had their school uniforms pressed, their lunches packed, and their evenings filled with bedtime stories. But beneath the calm efficiency, a subtle discontent brewed. It wasn't a grand rebellion, not an outright challenge to Kayode's choices, but a growing internal monologue of 'what ifs' and 'if only'. She would watch Kayode hunched over his spreadsheets, his brow furrowed in concentration, and a part of her would resent his singular focus, his apparent immunity to the everyday discomforts weighing her down. She yearned for him to see, to acknowledge the quiet sacrifices she was making, the emotional toll of this uprooting. But his gaze was fixed firmly on the horizon, on the promised land, and she felt increasingly stranded in the less-than-tranquil present.

The subtle shift began to show in small ways. Her smiles, once effortless and genuine, sometimes felt strained, as if a performance. The questions she posed to Kayode about their progress were no longer solely driven by curiosity but laced with an unspoken plea for reassurance and acknowledgement of her own burgeoning anxieties. She started to notice, with a prickle of envy, the carefully curated social media feeds of friends back home. Holidays were posted with dazzling regularity – sun-drenched beaches, vibrant city breaks, glamorous gatherings. Some of these posts were accompanied by captions that spoke of the "freedom" of single parenting, the "joy" of navigating life on one's own terms, a subtle but pointed jab at the constraints of partnered life, and by extension, at her own current reality.

It was insidious, this creeping comparison. A friend, newly divorced and radiating an almost defiant independence, posted a picture of herself sipping cocktails at a rooftop bar, her caption a triumphant declaration of self-reliance. Amina felt a sting, a sharp, unpleasant twist of longing. Was this what she was missing? This unburdened freedom. She knew, intellectually, that these online portrayals were often carefully constructed facades, highlight reels of lives that undoubtedly had their own share of struggles. Yet the images seeped in, planting seeds of doubt and discontent. The carefully crafted narrative of their move, the shared dream of a better future, felt increasingly like a burden she was carrying alone, while others, it seemed, were flitting through life with a privileged lightness.

She found herself gravitating towards online forums and groups for expatriates, initially seeking practical advice. But soon, the conversations veered into shared grievances and a collective airing of frustrations. Stories of homesickness, cultural misunderstandings, and the sheer effort required to build a new life from scratch resonated deeply. There was comfort in shared misery, a validation of her own feelings of overwhelm. She began spending more time scrolling through these digital spaces, absorbing the collective sighs of those navigating similar transitions. It was a double-edged sword, offering solace while reinforcing the narrative of hardship.

A particular incident brought this internal conflict into sharp relief. Maya had a school play approaching, a small role she was excited about. Amina had spent hours helping her practise her lines and carefully stitching a makeshift costume from scraps of fabric. On the day of the performance, Kayode was unexpectedly called at work and asked to take on an extra shift. Kayode agreed. He was already imagining how the additional income would help with home expenses and how Amina would be proud of him for earning it.

Amina went alone, her heart filled with a mix of pride in Maya and a familiar sense of being slightly out of sync with the effortless pairings around her. Other mothers arrived with their husbands, a small knot of fathers beaming from the back of the hall. Amina found herself standing slightly apart, a solitary figure in a sea of couples. When Maya spotted her, her face lit up, and after the performance, she rushed into her arms, her small voice full of breathless recounting of the performance. But the earlier sense of being an incomplete unit lingered, a faint shadow cast by the perceived completeness of others.

She began to withdraw, not from Kayode or the children, but from the relentless pursuit of integration. The effort to forge new friendships, join clubs, and actively participate in the wider community began to feel exhausting. In a way, it was easier to retreat into the familiar rhythms of her own home, to focus on the small, controllable universe of her family. This wasn't the easy life she had imagined. Still, perhaps she rationalised, it was a different kind of strength, a quiet resilience born not of grand adventures but of enduring the everyday. The carefully curated image of an easier life was dissolving, not into despair but into a more complex reality, one where impatience was slowly beginning to hide initial astonishment, and where the fog of London felt less like a romantic veil and more like a persistent, damp reminder of the distance she had travelled.

The seeds of doubt, sown by the relentless greyness and the sting of comparison, were beginning to sprout, quietly, persistently, in the fertile ground of her unmet expectations. She was still committed, still loving, but the unalloyed enthusiasm of those first few weeks had given way to a more sober, more realistic assessment of the long, arduous path that lay ahead.

UNSPOKEN EXPECTATIONS

The carefully constructed edifice of their new life in London, so diligently built by Kayode's unwavering optimism, was beginning to show hairline cracks, not from external pressures but from an internal conflict that was steadily growing within Amina. It wasn't a loud, dramatic rupture but a subtle, pervasive shift, like the slow erosion of a coastline by an insistent tide. While Kayode remained firmly anchored to his vision of professional advancement and financial security, Amina found herself grappling with the unspoken realities that began to redefine her understanding of partnership and progress. The grand narrative of a shared future, where both partners would contribute to a flourishing new chapter, was encountering the more complex, sometimes contradictory currents of ingrained cultural expectations and the subtle reordering of roles within the domestic sphere.

Back in Lagos, the concept of marriage had always felt more fluid, more intuitively understood. While Kayode, even then, had been the primary breadwinner, there had been a tacit acknowledgement that Amina's contributions to the household – her acumen in managing their finances, her relentless efforts in nurturing their children's education and well-being, her active role in supporting his career through social engagements and a constant, unwavering presence – were invaluable. These were not quantifiable metrics of financial gain but essential pillars on which their life together was built. The notion of "contribution" extended far beyond the salary slip, encompassing emotional, social, and domestic labour that was deeply respected and understood, if not always explicitly acknowledged in monetary terms. There was an unspoken equality, a recognition that the family's success was a collective endeavour, each member playing a vital, if different, part.

Here, however, the landscape of expectation seemed subtly, almost imperceptibly, reshaped. The initial conversations about Amina potentially seeking employment had been framed by Kayode as a shared ambition to accelerate their financial ascent, provide her with personal fulfilment and a sense of independence. He had spoken of it with an almost professorial air, outlining the benefits of a dual-income household, faster savings accumulation, and greater opportunities for their children. And Amina, too, had embraced this vision, seeing it as an extension of her capabilities, a chance to engage her mind and skills in a new environment, and a contribution to their collective prosperity. The idea that she would eventually work and that her income would be an integral part of their financial planning felt like a natural progression.

Yet as the weeks bled into months and Amina began exploring employment options, a different undercurrent began to make itself known. It wasn't in Kayode's words, which remained encouraging and supportive, but in subtle shifts in his interactions, in the way he sometimes spoke about their finances, and in the unspoken assumptions that began to colour their domestic discussions. The idea of her earning money had seamlessly integrated into his existing framework of financial responsibility, a framework perhaps still shaped mainly by the traditional male-controlled structures she had left behind.

For instance, there were casual remarks about household expenses. When discussing the cost of groceries or utilities, Kayode would sometimes say, "Once you start earning, we can really begin to save," or "Your salary will cover the children's extracurricular activities." These statements, while perhaps intended to highlight the financial benefits of her eventual employment, also carried an implicit weight. They suggested that her future income was earmarked for specific, often supplementary, expenses rather than being seen as an equal contribution to the family's overall financial stability. It was as if her potential earnings were a bonus, a means to enhance their comfort, rather than a fundamental part of their shared economic foundation.

This was a stark contrast to the understanding of financial partnership back home. There, if Amina had managed the household budget from her own earnings from a small business or investments, it was understood that this was her domain, and any surplus would be pooled or used for shared family goals. But if Kayode's salary was the primary source, her management of those funds was seen as a crucial act of stewardship, a vital contribution to the family's well-being, not merely an auxiliary function. Here, the emphasis seemed to shift from stewardship to a more direct, quantifiable contribution, with her worth, in part, tied to the pay cheque she would eventually bring home.

The unspoken expectation extended beyond the monetary. The division of labour within the home began to feel subtly imbalanced, particularly as Amina's search for employment intensified and, concurrently, her exploration of the London landscape. Kayode, consumed by his demanding job and meticulous planning for their future, often returned home late.

While he was not unsupportive, his engagement with domestic tasks seemed to diminish; his exhaustion was frequently cited as a reason for his reduced participation. Amina, on the other hand, found herself shouldering the bulk of childcare, cooking, cleaning, and the relentless demands of maintaining a household. This was, to some extent, the reality in Lagos as well, but there it was understood as her primary role, complemented by domestic help they could no longer afford. Here, however, there was the added layer of her impending employment, which heightened the urgency of her domestic duties, as if she needed to prove her capacity to manage both a home and a career before she even secured a job.

The pressure was not obvious, but it was deep. She began to feel a silent scrutiny, a subconscious assessment of her ability to juggle domestic responsibilities with the prospect of professional engagement. When she expressed her fatigue or her desire for Kayode to take on more, the response, while never dismissive, often circled back to his own workload, his own stress, and the larger goal they were working towards. The implicit message was that his efforts, as the primary financial provider and architect of their future, were of a different magnitude, requiring a greater allowance for his own needs and limitations. Her exhaustion and need for respite seemed to be viewed through a lens that prioritised her current non-earning status and the expectation that she would continue to manage the domestic sphere with quiet efficiency until her professional life officially began.

This was a subtle but significant departure from the dynamic back home. In Lagos, while Kayode was the primary breadwinner, there were moments, especially at weekends or during periods of less intense work, when he would readily step in, take the children out, or help with household chores, not out of obligation but out of a natural inclination to share the load and be present with his family. His participation was not a concession but a given. Here, his fatigue felt like a more permanent state, and his absences, due to work or social obligations related to his career, left Amina often to navigate the evening routine alone, the children's demands a constant tide against her own dwindling energy.

The perceived equality, a cornerstone of their shared vision, began to feel like a theoretical construct rather than a lived reality. The idea that, once she was earning, they would be equal partners in both contribution and responsibility was losing ground to a more traditional interpretation of roles, in which the man's career and well-being took precedence. The woman's efforts, both domestic and potentially professional, were seen as augmenting his primary role. This was not a conscious decision on Kayode's part; he knew. He was a product of his upbringing and of a society where these distinctions, though evolving, were still deeply embedded. But for Amina, who had envisioned a more modern, more equitable partnership, the realisation was disquieting.

She found herself constantly comparing their situation with that of some of their friends in Lagos, both those who had migrated and those who remained. She would recall conversations with friends whose husbands, even while holding demanding jobs, were actively involved in childcare, shared cooking duties, and ensured that their wives also had the space and time to pursue their own ambitions. There were a sense of mutual respect and a shared understanding that a successful partnership required a genuine sharing of burdens, not just a theoretical division of labour. Here, the "foggy shores" seemed not just a meteorological phenomenon but a metaphor for the obscuring of clear partnership lines and the blurring of expectations that left her feeling increasingly adrift.

The sting of comparison, initially directed at the curated lives of friends back home, now turns inwards, focusing on perceived discrepancies in her own marital dynamic. She misses the easy camaraderie she and Kayode once shared, the spontaneous conversations where they would brainstorm solutions to household dilemmas together. Now, their discussions about finances and responsibilities often feel like negotiations, with unspoken concessions and a subtle power imbalance. It is as if the very act of her seeking employment had inadvertently shifted the ground beneath them, creating a new set of unspoken rules she hadn't anticipated.

This growing unease was compounded by the sheer economic pressure of their new life. The cost of living, as she had already keenly felt, was a constant concern. While Kayode managed their finances with almost surgical precision, his careful budgeting and earnest explanations of their expenditure did not dispel the underlying tension that permeated their discussions. Every decision, from the cereal brand they bought to the frequency with which they ate out, was subjected to his rigorous scrutiny. While this frugality was necessary, it also meant that any perceived deviation, any suggestion of waste, was met with a quiet but firm reminder of their financial goals.

In this context, Amina's income became a focal point not only for accelerating their savings but also for easing immediate financial pressures. The unspoken expectation was that her salary would not merely add to their collective wealth but also serve as a buffer against daily anxieties, a source of funds that could ease some of the immediate financial strain. This was a heavier burden than she had imagined. It wasn't just about contributing to a shared future but also about providing immediate relief and serving as a financial safety net for their present.

She began to feel the weight of this unspoken expectation in the subtle ways Kayode would mention the rising costs of their children's upcoming needs – a new school uniform, a potential school trip, and the ever-increasing price of children's footwear. While these were legitimate concerns, their mention often felt like a gentle nudge, a subtle reminder of the financial responsibilities awaiting her. It wasn't an accusation, but a quiet framing of her future role as a provider, a solver of immediate financial puzzles. The challenge, she realised, lay in navigating these unspoken expectations without causing resentment or discord. She was not one to shy away from hard work or responsibility. Her life in Lagos had been a testament to her dedication and resilience. But she had also envisioned a partnership where effort and contribution were mutually acknowledged and shared, where the pressures were borne together, not disproportionately assigned based on outdated gender roles or the mere absence of a pay cheque.

The initial excitement of their move had been built on a foundation of shared dreams and a belief in a modern, equitable future. Now, as she took her first tentative steps towards realising her own professional ambitions, she was confronted with the reality that the foundations of their partnership, and the unspoken expectations that underpinned it, were being tested in ways she had not anticipated, here, on these foggy shores. The cultural differences were not merely academic observations; they were the very fabric of their daily lives, subtly reshaping their perceptions of each other and the roles they were expected to play.

CHAPTER 3

CRACKS IN THE FOUNDATION

BILL SHOCK

The reality of living in London hit home when the post arrived. Instead of birthday cards or letters from home, it brought reminders of new responsibilities. Back in Lagos, Kayode was used to steady, predictable expenses—mostly rent, food, and the occasional treat. Now he faced a stack of official envelopes. He knew London would be costly. He had read articles, listened to podcasts, and spoken with friends who had moved before him. Still, nothing had prepared him for just how constant and varied household expenses would be in the UK.

Mail arrived: utility bills from British Gas, E.ON, Thames Water, and the dreaded Council Tax. Kayode, weary but determined, collected them for his methodical sorting. Amid the children's boisterous morning, Amina found solace in their demands. At the kitchen table, tea in hand, he began opening the envelopes. The revelation in the gas bill struck him. The figures, a staggering sum, dwarfed his estimates, leaving him bewildered. Lagos's utility costs, once seemingly burdensome, now appeared negligible by comparison. Here, even basic needs exacted a significant toll. He contrasted this with their modest Ikoyi abode, where monthly utilities were an insignificant expense. This bill, however, signalled a far more serious financial predicament.

The electricity bill was another surprise. Kayode remembered his cousin's advice from Manchester about saving energy—turning off lights and using energy-efficient bulbs. Even so, the amount was much higher than he had expected. Seeing the total, he felt uneasy, realising this was not just a one-off cost but a regular, heavy expense.

Water had never seemed like a significant expense before. Although the bill was smaller than the others, it still added up. Everyday things like showers, laundry, cooking, and even the occasional car wash slowly eroded their savings.

Council Tax was new to them. It was a large payment for local services, based on the value of their home. This single bill was larger than all their monthly utility bills in Nigeria. Even in the warm kitchen, Kayode felt a chill. Their early optimism began to fade.

Their rented house was simple but met their needs. It wasn't fancy, but it was safe and clean. Still, just living there was expensive. They had planned for rent, food, travel, school, and a few small pleasures, but rising utility bills were an unexpected strain.

He remembered his father's advice from Lagos about saving for emergencies and planning. Kayode thought he had been careful, saving and making detailed plans. But the UK's financial challenges changed what counted as a necessity and forced them to be even more disciplined with money.

Amina entered the kitchen, a soft smile on her face as she surveyed the remnants of the breakfast rush. "Everything all right, Kayode?" she asked, her voice a gentle melody that had always soothed his anxieties.

He forced a smile, trying to suppress the nascent sense of dismay. "Yes, darling, just... sorting out some of the bills." He gestured towards the papers scattered across the table.

Amina's smile faltered at the sight of the official envelopes. The abstract concept of higher expenses had become a daunting reality. Preoccupied with settling the children, finding her footing, and her own career prospects, she'd overlooked the tangible costs of managing a household.

"Oh," she murmured, her voice hushed. Picking up an envelope, she read the bold print. "Utility bills, I gather."
"Yes," Kayode replied, his voice tenser than he intended. He usually prided himself on staying calm and handling money problems. But seeing these numbers shook him, making him doubt how prepared and resourceful he thought he was.

Amina sat, her gaze now fixed on the bills. Her innate grasp of numbers, refined by years of managing their Lagos budget even when Kayode's earnings were their sole support, came to the fore. She quickly calculated, comparing the figures with their budget. The shortfall was stark. "Kayode," she began, her voice measured, "these are... significantly higher than we anticipated, aren't they?"
He nodded, feeling uncomfortable about admitting it. "Yes. Especially the electricity and gas. I tried to estimate, but I was clearly too optimistic." He chose his words carefully, knowing he had underestimated the costs.

Amina reviewed the gas bill, focusing on the usage costs. They expected higher bills in winter, but even this early autumn bill, with mild weather, was already high. "We need to watch the thermostat," she said quietly. "And not heat empty rooms." She was already thinking about how they would have to be careful with their comfort to save money.

Her gaze shifted to the Council Tax notice. Although aware of its existence, she was struck by the concrete figure. "This Council Tax," she stated, concern colouring her tone, "is substantial. And it's annual. We'll need to divide it by twelve for the monthly burden." A pen and notepad appeared. Even before her job was confirmed, even before her earnings were factored into their finances, their outgoings loomed as a daunting obstacle.

Kayode watched Amina, feeling both impressed and a little defeated. She was already thinking of solutions, while he was still reeling from the shock. He knew there would be challenges, but he hadn't expected to face such severe financial problems so soon. He had thought they would have more time to adjust.

"I thought we had set aside enough for utilities," he said, frustration in his voice—not at Amina, but at the situation. "I expected them to be higher, but this..." He stopped, gesturing towards the bills on the table.

Amina placed her hand on Kayode's arm, trying to comfort him. "It's a big change from Lagos, Kayode. I get it. But we'll get through this. We always do." She wanted to reassure him, but they both knew it would require more sacrifice and planning than they had anticipated.

She frowned as she added up the numbers. Just utilities and Council Tax took up a large part of their monthly income, even before rent, food, transport, and other essentials. Their hope for quick financial progress now felt distant. The strong future Kayode had imagined now seemed shaky.

"Look," Amina said, tapping the notepad. "With stringent energy use and adjustments to our grocery shopping, we can manage. But our savings won't grow as we hoped, at least not in these first months."

This was what worried Kayode most. His whole plan for moving was based on saving a lot for future investments and business growth. Now, these bills made it feel as if the quick journey he had hoped for was turning into a long, tiring struggle.

"It's more than just savings, Amina," he admitted, his voice low. "It's the principle. My projections were far off. My research feels… inadequate." He ran a hand through his hair, agitated. "We need more than just essentials; we need a buffer. What about car trouble or unexpected needs for the children?"

Bills used to be just paperwork, but now they feel harsh. It was clear their careful financial plans had been too optimistic, maybe even naive. Their bright ideas about London were meeting the harsh reality of everyday costs. The high cost of just getting by was a loud wake-up call.

Watching Amina stay focused and practical, Kayode felt grateful for her steady approach. She was already thinking of ways to manage the new expenses, while he regretted not planning better. He had been the one with the big ideas for moving, but now those plans were being tested by the reality of their bills.

"We have to be more careful now," he said, sounding a bit more confident. "Every penny matters. Maybe we should look at our spending in other areas, too. No more eating out for now. And maybe we can find cheaper ways to get around."

Amina agreed. "Yes. When I start working, it will help a lot, but until then, we have to be very careful." She knew her future income wouldn't just help them save—it would be needed to cover their basic needs right away.

The bills made it clear there was a big gap between their dreams and their current situation. It wasn't just about the money—it showed how hard daily life could be. This was the first real sign that things might not go as planned. Their strong will would have to be matched by new skills and resilience. The worry about Amina's future, once small, now felt much bigger as they faced these numbers. The hope for plenty was fading, replaced by the urgent need to manage their costs. London's financial reality had left its mark.

CHILDREN'S QUITE OBSERVATION

The children sensed the quiet tension in their new London home, even if they didn't fully understand it. Maya, always observant, noticed her father's shoulders droop a little more after certain letters arrived. She saw her mother's smile, once bright and easy, sometimes fade, as if a candle had been blown out. There were no loud arguments like those back in Lagos, just a steady, uneasy feeling that filled the house.

Mornings used to be filled with playful noise and excitement, but now they felt different, quieter. The sound of envelopes being opened, once unremarkable, now made everyone uneasy. Kayode tried to act usual, quickly putting the letters away and saying, "Just sorting out some things, children," though his tense jaw gave him away. Amina would distract herself with chores or tidying up toys. Still, the children could sense that something was wrong.

At seven, Maya watched her mother fold her father's shirts with careful, almost robotic movements. Amina seemed more deliberate in everything she did, holding herself together with effort. Maya noticed that her mother sometimes paused, tracing the edge of a teacup and staring off, especially after her father dealt with the mail. Maya was starting to understand these silent signals of worry. Kofi, just five, could sense the mood in the house. His parents' worries weighed heavily, making him less playful than before. His games in the garden, once loud and full of adventure, grew quieter.

He spent more time lining up his toy cars, frowning in concentration, as if trying to bring order to things. He often looked to Maya for comfort but usually found her just as quiet as he was. Trips to the local park, once full of excitement, now felt different. The children still enjoyed the open spaces and the playground, but there was a sense of worry mixed in. Sometimes, Maya would pause to listen to her parents talking quietly on a bench. She didn't always catch what they said, but she recognised the serious tone—

the same one that led to her mother's sighs or her father's long silences.

One sunny afternoon, Maya and Kofi were busy building a sandcastle when you overheard their parents talking about the electricity bill. Maya, always listening, caught snatches of the conversation. Her mother said, "...much higher than we expected," sounding worried. Her father replied, "...have to be more careful," his voice tired in a way Maya was starting to recognise, his small face etched with concern. He nudged Maya with his elbow. "Mama sounds sad," he whispered.

Maya nodded, smoothing the top of their sandcastle. "It's the bills, Kofi," she said softly. "Dad says London is very expensive." She didn't really know what "expensive" meant, but she knew it was something that made her parents stop smiling and speak in hushed voices.

Later that week, while Amina was laying out the school uniforms, she saw Maya carefully folding her own clothes, copying her mother's way. "What are you doing, darling?" Amina asked, smiling gently.

Maya looked up, serious. "I'm making sure they're neat, Mummy, so they don't get worn out, and so they don't cost too much to wash."

Amina's smile faded for a moment. She knelt and hugged Maya. "That's very thoughtful, my love," she said, trying to sound cheerful. "But don't worry about that. Mummy will take care of it."

As she held her daughter, Amina felt a pang of guilt, realising Maya was already picking up on their worries.

The children's playtime, once an uninhibited exploration of their surroundings, was now peppered with moments of introspection. They would sit side by side, their knees touching, in a comfortable silence that had evolved from shared companionship into shared playtime. The children, once carefree, were now quieter and more thoughtful. They would sit together in silence, not just as friends but as kids who understood each other's worries. They watched other children play loudly and sometimes joined in, but part of them stayed on the sidelines, careful and watchful. They were learning to hold back, waiting to see how things felt before letting themselves have fun. "Do we have to give money even if we don't go to the park every day?"

Kayode paused, the analogy suddenly feeling inadequate, too simplistic. He looked at Maya's earnest face, the genuine confusion in her eyes. He saw in her a reflection of his own struggle to reconcile the abstract demands of this new country with the concrete realities of their lives. "Yes, Maya," he said, his voice gentler than usual. "It's like… a way of helping to pay for the things everyone uses, such as the roads, the streetlights, even the libraries."

Amina, who had been listening from the doorway, stepped forward. She saw Maya's eyebrow contract further and the subtle tremble of her lower lip. It was not just the financial aspect that was troubling Maya; it was the inherent unfairness, the sense that they were being asked to pay for things they didn't fully understand and for services they hadn't explicitly requested.

"It's a bit like paying for the air we breathe, isn't it?" Amina interjected, trying to soften the blow. "We don't see it, but it's there, helping everything work."

Maya considered this, her gaze shifting from her father to her mother. She was a child of logic, and while the analogy was more poetic, it didn't fully address her nascent sense of unease. She observed her parents' careful explanations and their attempts to frame these financial burdens as necessary and equitable. But she also saw the underlying strain, the way they had to pause, search for words, and carefully curate their explanations.

Their bedtime stories, once fantastical journeys to faraway lands, began to incorporate themes of resilience and careful management. Amina might read a tale about a resourceful little mouse who learned to save every crumb, or Kayode might recount a fable about a king who knew the importance of budgeting his kingdom's treasury. These were not conscious decisions to infuse their children with their own anxieties, but rather a subconscious filtering of their experiences, a way of processing their own struggles by translating them into lessons for their young ones.

The children's quiet observation extended to the very rhythm of their home. They noticed how promptly the lights were switched off and the heating adjusted, with newfound vigilance. They saw their parents forgo small pleasures, such as buying an extra treat at the shop or ordering a takeaway. These were not sacrifices explicitly explained to them as such, but the absence of these small joys was noted, a subtle deprivation that spoke volumes.

One Saturday, as Amina carefully portioned out their groceries, ensuring each item would last as long as possible, Maya watched her with wide eyes. "Mummy, can we buy more biscuits?" she asked, pointing to the almost-empty packet.

Amina sighed, a soft, almost inaudible sound. "Not today, darling. We have to make these last. We have to be very careful with our money."

Maya's gaze dropped to the floor. She understood the words, but she also understood the tone and the subtle shift in her mother's disposition. It wasn't just about biscuits; it was about a curtailment, a necessary restraint. She didn't complain or protest. Instead, she quietly picked up a piece of apple from the fruit bowl, a readily available, cost-free alternative. It was a small gesture, but it spoke volumes about her growing understanding of their evolving circumstances.

Kofi, too, was adapting. His requests for new toys or specific sweets became fewer. He often chose to play with his existing toys or invent new games using everyday objects. When asked what he wanted for his upcoming birthday, he hesitated, then said, "Just a drawing of a big blue whale, please, Dad. And maybe a new book to read." It was a far cry from the elaborate toy wish lists he might have conjured in Lagos, a testament to his quiet recalibration.

The children's innocence was not entirely shattered. The wonder of London still held them captive. The novelty of the red buses, the vastness of the parks, and the sheer diversity of faces and voices on the streets – these were still potent sources of fascination. Yet woven into their exploration was a new layer of awareness. They were not just tourists in this new land; they were also sensitive barometers of their parents' emotional and financial well-being.

They were learning to read subtle cues, navigate unspoken tensions, and exist within the quiet hum of their parents' anxieties. The hushed arguments, when they did occur, were particularly impactful. Maya would sometimes hear raised voices from the main bedroom, her father's frustration and her mother's firm yet pleading tone. She would lie in her bed, her heart pounding, and pull her duvet tighter, as if seeking a physical barrier against the emotional storm. Kofi would often cry out in his sleep on those nights, his small body restless.

The children, though separated by age, were united in their quiet observation and shared sensitivity to the cracks forming in the foundation of their new life. Their wonder at London remained, but a growing understanding tempered it, showing that the smiles and assurances of their parents were sometimes a carefully constructed facade, a shield against a reality they were only beginning to comprehend, a reality that was slowly, inevitably, dimming the bright promise of their new beginning. Their innocent observation was not a passive act; it was an active process of adaptation, of learning to live within the subtle yet profound shifts in their family's emotional landscape.

EARNING POWER AND EXPECTED PAYOUTS

The anxiety that had accompanied the initial job search began to recede, replaced by a more insidious worry. Kayode had done it. He had navigated the complex application processes, the nerve-wracking interviews, and the endless waiting. He had secured a position, a tangible anchor amid the currents of his new life. The congratulatory calls from friends and family back home, filled with relief and renewed hope, had been a balm to his weary spirit. He had proven, to himself and to them, that the sacrifices were not in vain.

But the feeling of relief was fleeting, a transient sensation. A looming cloud quickly hid a warm sun. The salary, when it finally appeared in his bank account, was a number that looked respectable on paper. It represented stability, a steady flow of income he had yearned for. Yet as he began to dissect the practical implications, the sheer weight of it, in relation to the relentless demands of London life, became apparent. The initial optimism, the vision of saving for a down payment on a small flat or even, dare he dream, a holiday back home, began to fray at the edges.

The cost of his rented accommodation, a modest two-bedroom flat in a less-than-fashionable part of town, consumed a significant portion of his income. Then there were the utilities – electricity, gas, and water – each bill arriving with disquieting regularity and an ever-increasing figure. The Council Tax, a concept that still felt alien and burdensome, added another substantial deduction. Groceries, once a relatively manageable expense, now required careful budgeting, constant price comparisons, and an almost militant avoidance of impulse purchases. Even the simple act of commuting to work, the daily train fare, represented a considerable outgoing.

He found himself meticulously calculating, his mind a ledger of debits and credits. He would compare the cost of a loaf of bread in one supermarket with another, a task he'd never had to undertake with such diligence before. He'd analyse public transport routes, looking for the cheapest, often the longest, way to get from A to B. The casual ease with which he used to spend, the freedom he'd taken for granted, was a distant memory. Every pound spent felt significant, a slight erosion of his hard-won stability.

Amina, ever observant, noticed the subtle shifts in her husband. She saw him pore over bank statements late into the night. She heard the sighs that escaped him when another bill arrived, and the quiet frustration in his voice when he spoke of unexpected expenses. Her initial joy at his securing employment had been immense, but she was not naive. She understood that in this new land, the promise of a better life was intricately linked to financial security, and that security was proving to be a more elusive quarry than they had anticipated.

One evening, as Kayode meticulously planned their meals for the week, trying to stretch their budget, Amina sat beside him, her gaze fixed on the spreadsheet he had spread across the kitchen table. "Kayode," she began, her voice soft yet firm, "this salary… It's good, it's stable, but it feels like it disappears before we even see it."

He looked up, a tired smile on his face. "I know, Amina. London is relentless. It demands. Every little thing costs. We are managing, though. We are making it work."

"Managing is not thriving, Kayode," she countered, her tone sharpening slightly. "We came here with dreams, not just to survive but to build something. To give the children a better future, yes, but also to have some semblance of comfort and security for ourselves." She picked up a bill from the pile. "This is for utilities. This is for rent. This is for food. Where is the money for anything else? For that new washing machine, we need what? For building up a little savings for emergencies? For even a small indulgence now and then?"

Kayode sighed, weariness seeping back into his voice. "I am working hard, Amina. This is what I earn. We must be realistic. We have to prioritise."
"And what are we prioritising?" she pressed, her eyes meeting his. "Are we prioritising the immediate demands of survival, or are we building towards a future where we are not constantly just treading water? Your earnings, Kayode, are essential. They keep the roof over our heads and put food on our table. That is their primary purpose now. But what about our aspirations? What about the things we wanted for ourselves, for our life here?"

Her words, though spoken with affection, carried a weight of unspoken expectation. It was as if she had drawn a clear line, defining the boundaries of his salary. In her eyes, his income was now irrevocably tied to the upkeep of their household and the necessities of their life in London. The dreams of personal investment, discretionary spending, and building personal wealth beyond the family's immediate needs seemed relegated to a distant, unattainable future.

"I understand, Amina," he said, his voice tinged with a hint of defensiveness. "But we are in a new country. It takes time to adjust and to build up our finances. We can't expect to have everything at once. This job is a good start."

"A start, yes," she conceded. "But a start that needs to be managed with a clear vision. Your earnings, Kayode, are the foundation. And a foundation needs to be strong, not just for the walls and the roof, but for the rooms we want to build within it. I see you stressing over every penny. I see you looking at things you'd like to buy, but then putting them back. That is not how we should be living, not permanently."

She paused, then continued, her voice laced with a new assertiveness. "We need to be more strategic. As it stands, your salary is for survival and the children's needs. I agree. But we also need to allocate a portion, however small, to growth. To our future. That means making conscious decisions, not just about what we spend, but about what we save and how we invest. Perhaps I should take more control of the budget. I can ensure the essential expenses are covered, and then we can look at how best to allocate the rest. We can't afford for your earnings to be just a constant cycle of bills and immediate needs. There has to be more."

He heard the unspoken implication. Amina, who had always been the more frugal of the two, the meticulous planner of household expenses, was now stepping forward, not just as a partner in managing their finances, but as the one who would dictate their allocation. It wasn't a criticism of his earning capacity, but a clear statement of priorities, a redirection of his income's purpose. His salary was no longer solely his to manage, with aspirations for personal growth and investment alongside family needs. It was, in essence, being designated for the family's immediate and long-term security, with his own personal ambitions taking a backseat.

The relief of employment had been replaced by the weight of responsibility, a responsibility that now extended beyond simply earning a living. It was about managing that income to meet the pragmatic demands of their new life in London. At the same time, Amina, with her growing conviction, would ensure that the family's financial well-being, in its broadest sense, was secured. The cracks in the foundation were not just economic; they were also about the evolving dynamics of their partnership and the subtle renegotiation of roles and expectations in the face of the relentless pressures of their new reality. The dream of a comfortable life was being redefined, not by abundance, but by the careful, sometimes contentious rationing of their resources.

THE SEED OF RESENTMENT

The weight of his salary, once a symbol of success and relief, now pressed down on Kayode like a physical burden. It was a tangible manifestation of the expectations that had followed him across the ocean, expectations that now seemed to eclipse the very dreams they were meant to fuel. He'd secured the job, the steady income, the anchor he'd so desperately needed. Yet instead of solidifying his newfound ground, it felt as though his feet were sinking deeper into a mire of ever-increasing expenses. The meticulous budgeting, the constant calculations, the vigilant scanning of supermarket shelves for the cheapest option – these were not the acts of a man building a prosperous future, but of a man perpetually on the brink of scarcity.

He remembered the conversations back home, the hopeful pronouncements about what his earnings would unlock. Not just survival, but a tangible improvement, a step towards the aspirations he and Amina had nurtured. He had envisioned a life where they weren't constantly chasing the next bill, where there was room for the occasional splurge, for the small comforts that made life not just bearable but enjoyable. He saw himself contributing to something larger than the immediate upkeep of their household, perhaps investing, or, in the distant future, finding a way to support causes in Nigeria close to his heart. But London's relentless demands had a way of shrinking those expansive dreams into a narrow, utilitarian corridor.

Amina's pragmatic approach, while undeniably necessary, felt like a subtle redirection of his efforts. Her meticulous management of the budget, her careful allocation of every pound, was not just about financial prudence; it was beginning to feel like a quiet appropriation. When she spoke of allocating portions of his salary, it was no longer about shared decision-making but about her taking the reins and defining the purpose of the money he worked so hard to earn. It was as if his role as the primary provider, the one who wrestled income from the city's grasp, was being reduced to a mere conduit, a source of funds that would then be channelled and controlled by her strategic vision.

He found himself observing her with a new, almost detached curiosity. Her initial joy at his securing employment had faded. Her focus had narrowed, sharpened by the daily grind of their financial reality. She saw the bills, the expenses, the immediate needs, and her mind, ever logical, was programmed to address them with unflinching efficiency. This efficiency, however, was beginning to feel like a cage, not just for their money but for his spirit. He felt a growing disconnect between the man who earned the money and the man who had to account for every minute of its expenditure.

The conversations had shifted, too. Discussions of budgets, savings goals, and the rising cost of bread had replaced the easy camaraderie and shared exploration of their new life. When he tried to speak of his nascent ideas, potential side projects, or even a small personal indulgence, he was met with gentle but firm redirection back to the immediate financial realities. "We can't afford that right now, Kayode" became a frequent refrain, a polite but effective dismissal of his aspirations. He began to feel like an employee in his own life, his performance measured not by his dedication or the quality of his work, but by the surplus he could generate after all essential expenses were met.

He remembered a specific incident, a minor one in the grand scheme of things, yet one that had lodged itself in his mind. He'd seen a rather smart, but not exorbitant, watch in a shop window. It wasn't flashy, but it had a certain understated elegance, a reflection of the kind of man he aspired to be. He had considered it, a fleeting thought of rewarding himself for the relentless effort. When he mentioned it to Amina later, casually, as a distant possibility, her response had been immediate and unequivocal. "A watch, Kayode? We need to save for a new washing machine. That old one is on its last legs. A watch is a luxury we cannot justify right now." The way she said "luxury" felt like a judgment, a subtle accusation that his desires were frivolous, out of sync with their pressing needs.

This was the seed of resentment, a small, almost imperceptible thing that began to sprout in the fertile ground of his unspoken frustrations. It wasn't anger, not yet, but a quiet, simmering discontent. He was providing, sacrificing, and working harder than he ever had. He was enduring the loneliness of a new city, the cultural shifts, and the constant effort to adapt. And for what? To have his every earning scrutinised, his every potential indulgence dismissed as a luxury. He felt a growing sense of being unappreciated, his efforts reduced to mere numbers on a ledger, his sacrifices invisible beneath the weight of their financial obligations.

The freedom he had imagined, the liberation that financial independence was supposed to bring, felt like an illusion. Instead, he was tethered more tightly than ever, his life dictated by the relentless demands of a city that seemed designed to extract every last penny. The dream of a better future, once a beacon of hope, now felt like a distant mirage, receding further with every step he took. He was trapped, not by poverty, but by the very wealth he was striving to create.

The initial optimism had curdled, replaced by a sense of being trapped in a cage, with bars made of bills, and freedom measured by the dwindling balance in their bank account.

He found himself withdrawing, the spark of ambition dimming, replaced by weary resignation. The city that promised so much was slowly, insidiously stealing the joy from his efforts, leaving only a hollow echo of what he had hoped to achieve. He looked at Amina and saw not a partner in their shared journey, but a silent accountant, meticulously tallying his perceived failures against an ever-shifting standard of financial success. This was not the life they had envisioned; this was a slow erosion of spirit, a quiet surrender to London's relentless, unyielding grip on its economic reality.

CHAPTER 4
THE UNRAVILING PARTNERSHIP

THE FIRST ULTIMATUM

The evening air, which usually felt refreshing after a long day at the warehouse, now felt heavy with tension. Kayode stood by the window, looking out at the city lights, his mind full of worries. He had expected the usual budget talks and Amina's careful attention to every pound. Her practical approach was something he had always admired, helping them stay grounded in their new life. But lately, he felt a growing distance between his hard work and how she saw their finances, and that feeling was becoming harder to ignore.

He thought back over their conversation, remembering how Amina had gone through their expenses with her usual precision. This routine felt different tonight. He had casually mentioned wanting to buy a new shirt, since his work clothes were plain and he hoped to look a bit better. He tried to bring it up gently, not as a demand, but as a small wish for himself.

Amina's response had been swift, devoid of its usual gentle redirection. Her eyes, usually soft with concern or alight with shared ambition, had hardened, her voice taking on a tone he hadn't heard before. It was a tone that spoke not of shared challenges, but of clear obligations, of boundaries drawn in the sand. "A shirt, Kayode?" she had repeated, the words flat, almost dismissive. "Have you looked at the electricity bill lately? Or the rent increase that's due next month? These are not optional. We need to prioritise."

This time, there was no gentle "maybe later" or "let's see what we can do." Instead, Amina made a clear statement that left no room for discussion. Then she gave him a direct ultimatum, and its seriousness unsettled him.

"You need to contribute more," she'd said, her gaze unwavering, fixed on the spreadsheet as if it held the gospel of their survival. "This is your share for the bills. It needs to be there, in full, by the end of the week. No excuses."

Her words lingered, cold and final. "Your share." It wasn't about "our" expenses anymore. The sense of partnership was gone, replaced by a demand. Kayode had worked long hours, dealt with loneliness and homesickness, all to support their future. Now, he was being told that what he gave wasn't enough.

He thought about the dreams they once shared back in Nigeria—dreams of building a good life together and supporting each other. He had pictured them working as a team, each playing a part. But now, it felt like he was just being handed a bill, a demand for money, and a reminder of where he was falling short.

"But Amina," he had started, his voice a little hoarse, his mind scrambling for a coherent response. "I've been… I'm already putting everything I earn towards the bills. The extra shifts…"

She had cut him off, her expression unyielding. "Everything isn't enough, Kayode. The cost of living here. It's not what we expected. We need more. And that means you need to find a way to provide more."

Her voice showed no empathy or recognition of how hard he was already working. She stated what was needed, without any comfort. Kayode felt a sense of betrayal. Was this the same woman who had once held his hand with hope as they started this journey together? Was this the partner who had promised to face challenges by his side?

He tried to reason with her, to explain the limitations, the sheer impossibility of extracting more from a system that already demanded every ounce of his energy. "Where am I supposed to get more from, Amina? I work sixty hours a week. There are no more hours in the day."

Her response was a sigh, a sound of weary exasperation that pricked at his already raw nerves. "That's not my problem, Kayode. I'm telling you what needs to happen. We can't live like this. We need to maintain a certain standard. And that requires more money. If you can't provide it, then perhaps we need to reconsider"

The unspoken threat hung in the air, a chilling possibility that he dared not articulate, even to himself. Reconsider what? Their partnership? Their future together? The very fabric of the life they were trying to weave in this alien land.

A deep sense of loneliness came over him. Even in a city full of people, he felt utterly alone. The woman he loved had given him an ultimatum that seemed impossible to meet, and her coldness hurt him deeply. Their teamwork and shared journey felt broken. He no longer felt like a partner, but someone struggling to reach an impossible goal with nothing left to give.

He pulled back, her words stuck in his mind. "You need to contribute more." The phrase echoed in the quiet of their flat. It wasn't a request—it was a demand, making him feel like he wasn't enough. He wanted to defend himself, to talk about all he had done and given up, but he knew it wouldn't change anything. Amina had made up her mind, and things had changed.

He looked out at the city again. The lights seemed harsh and distant, almost mocking. He had come here hoping for a better life for himself and Amina, working hard and believing his efforts would matter. Now, that dream felt like it was falling apart, replaced by demands he couldn't meet. The hardest part was that these demands came from the person he thought would always support him. Their partnership, he realised, was starting to fall apart, not suddenly, but through this cold ultimatum.

He walked away from the window, the floorboards creaking softly under his weight, a testament to the solidity he had once believed their life possessed. Now, it felt as fragile as glass, and Amina's words had been the first, sharp blow. He found himself drawn to the small, worn armchair in the corner, a tangible reminder of simpler times, of a shared understanding that seemed to have evaporated into the London fog. He sank into it, the familiar contours offering little comfort.

The details of her demand were specific but conveyed a broader implication that overshadowed the individual sum. It wasn't just about a single bill; it was about a fundamental shift in their financial dynamic. "This is your share for the bills," she had said, her voice laced with an authority that surprised him. It implied a calculation, a judgment of his worth, his contribution, against some invisible benchmark of household necessity. He had always viewed their income as a joint resource, a pool from which they drew, together, to meet their needs. But her framing had fractured that shared pool into discrete portions, assigning him a specific, non-negotiable liability.

He tried to retrace the moments leading up to her pronouncement, to pinpoint the exact inflexion point where their conversation had veered into this stark demand. He recalled her earlier, almost casual, mention of the rising cost of their weekly grocery shop. He'd nodded, acknowledging the reality of it, a grim acceptance of London's inflationary grip. He'd even volunteered to try and find a cheaper supermarket, to make a memorable trip to a discount store on his day off, an offer that had been met with a swift, almost dismissive, "It won't make enough difference, Kayode."

Then, she had opened the spreadsheet. It wasn't the casual perusal of their finances they sometimes engaged in; this was a deliberate presentation. Her finger had traced lines, highlighting figures with an almost aggressive certainty. It was as if she had already made her decision, and the spreadsheet was merely the evidence she was presenting to justify it.

"The gas bill alone has gone up by twenty per cent," she had stated, her voice unnervingly steady. "And with the winter approaching, we can't afford to be frugal with heating. Then there's the council tax, which seems to be a constant upward climb. And our food expenses. It's simply unsustainable at the current rate."

He had listened, his own anxieties about their financial instability mirroring hers, but he had also felt a growing unease at the way she was presenting these facts. They were given not as shared challenges, but as a list of his failures to meet them adequately.

"I understand, Amina," he had replied, trying to keep his voice calm, to inject a note of reassurance. "We'll have to cut back on a few things. Perhaps we can postpone the new sofa for a while longer."

This had been the moment her gaze lifted, meeting his with an intensity that unnerved him. The gentle plea in his suggestion seemed to evaporate under the force of her directness. "Postponing isn't going to solve the problem, Kayode," she had said, her voice hardening. "We need a concrete solution. And the solution is that you need to contribute more."

The words, 'contribute more,' landed like stones. They were blunt, accusatory, and completely lacking in the collaborative spirit that had always defined their relationship. He felt a prickle of defensiveness, a desperate urge to explain that he was already doing everything he could, that his entire existence had been recalibrated around the sole purpose of earning and providing.

"Amina, I… I don't understand," he had stammered, his carefully constructed composure beginning to fray. "I work sixty hours a week. I send home as much as I possibly can after covering my own living expenses here. What more can I do?"

Her response was a sharp intake of breath, a sound of impatience. "The money you send home, Kayode, that's your 'share.' And it's not enough. The bills are piling up, and we're barely surviving. This isn't about 'sending home'; this is about meeting the demands of our life *here*. And your share of that is not adequate. You need to give us more."

'Us.' The word, in her mouth, seemed to demarcate him from the 'us,' as if he were an external entity whose financial obligations were being assessed. He felt a cold dread seep into his bones. He had imagined himself as the bedrock of their new life, the provider of security and stability. Now, he felt like a tenant being served an eviction notice for failing to meet his rent.

He remembered a conversation they'd had shortly after his arrival. Amina had been so proud, so relieved that he had secured a stable job. She had spoken of his earnings as a collective achievement, a testament to their shared resilience. "With your salary, Kayode," she had said, her eyes shining, "we can finally start building that future we talked about. We can save, we can plan. It's the start of something wonderful."

But the 'something wonderful' had morphed into this stark, impersonal demand. The chilling logic of budgetary necessity had replaced the warmth of their shared ambition. He felt a profound sense of disillusionment. He was in a foreign land, working a gruelling job, sacrificing his comfort and time, all for the promise of a better life. And now, the person who was supposed to be his partner in this pursuit had turned the pursuit itself into a source of accusation.

He tried to appeal to their shared past, to the understanding that had always guided them. "Amina, we've always managed things together. We've always discussed our finances. This feels different. It feels like an ultimatum."

She had met his gaze, her expression unreadable for a moment before settling back into a mask of resolve. "It is what it is, Kayode," she had said, her voice devoid of warmth. "The reality of living here demands it. You need to contribute more. This is your share of the bills. It needs to be done."

The finality in her tone was absolute. There was no room for debate, no allowance for his own struggles, his own sacrifices. He was presented with a unilateral decision that reshaped the very foundation of their partnership. He looked at her, searching for any flicker of the woman he knew, the woman who had shared his dreams, his fears, his hopes. But all he saw was a woman facing down a formidable financial reality, who, in the process, had drawn a line in the sand, demanding that he step across it.

He stood from the armchair, the worn fabric offering no solace. He felt a hollowness within him, a sense of profound loss that went beyond the financial. The dream he had chased across the ocean seemed to be disintegrating, not under the pressure of external circumstances but under the weight of a fractured partnership. The first ultimatum had been issued, a chilling indication of what was to come. He looked out at the indifferent city lights and, for the first time, felt truly alone.

THREATS OF EVICTION

The air in the small flat had grown thin, the silence between them not just an absence of sound but of unspoken accusations and the ghost of shared dreams. Kayode found himself pacing the worn rug, each step a silent question mark in the oppressive atmosphere. Amina sat at the small dining table, her posture rigid, her gaze fixed on something unseen beyond the window. He knew, with a certainty that chilled him more than the November air seeping through the ill-fitting window frames, that the conversation had irrevocably shifted. The ultimatum about his contribution, the demand that felt like a judgment on his very worth, had been merely the prelude. The main act, the truly terrifying end, was about to unfold.

"So," he began, his voice rough, unused to the charged silence. "You said… You said we need to reconsider." He braced himself, dreading the words he'd been dreading since she'd uttered them a moment ago. He had tried to steer the conversation away from that cliff, to pull it back into the familiar territory of shared problem-solving, but she had held firm. Her eyes, when they had met his earlier, had been devoid of the warmth he craved, replaced by a chilling pragmatism that felt alien.

Amina finally turned, her expression unreadable. He realised it was a mask she had perfected. "Yes, Kayode. We need to reconsider." Her voice was quiet, almost conversational, yet it carried the weight of a hammer blow. She didn't raise it, didn't shout, but the calculated calm was far more unnerving than any outburst. "This… this arrangement we have. It's not working."

Kayode's breath hitched. "Not working? Amina, we're trying. I'm trying. I told you I'm working as many hours as I possibly can. There isn't any more time to give." He gestured helplessly, his hands falling back to his sides as if defeated by an invisible force. "The job is demanding. It takes everything out of me."

She gave a short, humourless laugh. "Demanding. Yes, it is. But it's also not providing what we need, Kayode. Not what I need. We agreed this would be a step up—a better life. Frankly, Kayode, this isn't it. Not for me. Not for us, if you insist on clinging to this notion of 'us'."

The way she emphasised 'us' sent a fresh wave of unease through him. It was as if she were distancing herself, subtly but deliberately. "What do you mean, 'not for me'?" he asked, his voice barely a whisper. He feared the answer, but even more the silence.

"I mean," she continued, her gaze steady, unnervingly so, "that I am not prepared to live like this indefinitely. Skimping and saving for every little thing. Worrying about the next bill, the next rent increase. It's exhausting. And the primary reason for this struggle, Kayode, is the inadequacy of your contribution."

He flinched at the word 'inadequacy'. It was a brand, a scarlet letter seared into his soul. "My contribution? Amina, I'm sending home nearly everything I earn! After my rent, my food, my work travel, what is left? You know this. We've gone through the figures before." He tried to keep his voice even, to appeal to reason and to their shared history of financial transparency.

"The figures don't lie, Kayode," she said, her voice hardening. "And they tell me that, even with your 'extra hours,' your current income is not sufficient to sustain the life we were promised. The life I envisioned when we decided to come here." She paused, letting the implication hang in the air. "And if your earnings are not enough, perhaps… perhaps we need to explore other options."

Kayode's heart began to pound a frantic rhythm against his ribs. "Other options? What other options are there, Amina? I can't magic more money out of thin air. This job is the best I could find. The opportunities here are not as abundant as they told us." He remembered the glossy brochures, the promises of a land of opportunity, where hard work guaranteed prosperity. It now felt like a cruel joke.

Amina leaned forward, her eyes narrowing slightly. "Perhaps," she said, her voice dropping to a conspiratorial yet chilling tone, "perhaps the solution isn't about you earning more. Perhaps it's about finding someone who can."

The words hit him like a physical blow. He stumbled back, his hand instinctively reaching for the wall for support. "Someone who can? What are you saying, Amina? Are you saying you'd leave me for someone else?" The thought was so devastating, so utterly inconceivable, that he struggled to process it.

She offered a small, tight smile, devoid of mirth. "Don't be dramatic, Kayode. I'm merely stating the reality of our situation. If your financial contribution is the barrier to achieving the life we desire, then we must address it. And if you cannot overcome it, then I must find a way to move past it."

He stared at her, his mind reeling. This wasn't just about money anymore. It was about his worth, his value, his place in her life. "Amina, how can you… after everything? After all we've been through. Are you talking about leaving me? Because I can't earn enough?"

"I'm talking about survival, Kayode," she retorted, her voice sharpening. "I'm talking about the practicalities of life in this city. It's not a fairy tale. It's a constant struggle, and frankly, I'm tired of being the only one who seems to grasp the urgency. You seem content to get by. I want more than that. I deserve more than that." He felt a knot of fear tighten in his stomach. He knew from hushed conversations with other migrants of the desperate situations some found themselves in. Stories of people being exploited, of families torn apart by financial pressures. He had always believed he and Amina were strong enough to weather any storm. But now it seemed the storm was not external but internal.

"But… the thought of you leaving…" he began, his voice cracking. "Where would I go? I can barely afford this flat on my own. If you leave, what happens to me? I don't have anyone here, Amina. You are my anchor."

Amina's gaze softened, but not with empathy. It was more like a calculated assessment. "That, Kayode, is precisely the problem. You have made yourself entirely dependent. And now that dependence is becoming a burden."

He felt a cold dread seep into his bones. He understood, with horrifying clarity, what she was implying. She wasn't just threatening to leave; she was threatening to strip away his very foundation. "What… what do you mean, a burden?" he asked, his voice barely audible.

"I mean," she said, her voice taking on a chilling finality, "that if you cannot contribute sufficiently to our household, if your presence here, financially speaking, is a drain rather than a support, then perhaps… perhaps you cannot remain here."

The implication struck him with the force of a physical blow. Eviction. The word, unspoken yet powerfully present, echoed in the small room. For any migrant, the threat of losing one's home and becoming truly rootless in a foreign land was the ultimate terror. And Amina, the woman he loved, the woman he had risked everything for, was wielding that terror as a weapon.

"Evict me?" he choked out, the words tasting of ash. "You would… You would evict me?"

She looked away, her jaw tight. "I am not saying that, Kayode. I am saying we need to be realistic. If your financial situation does not improve rapidly, the current arrangement becomes untenable. I cannot afford to support both of us indefinitely on my current income, and your contribution is inadequate."

The carefully chosen words "current arrangement," "untenable," and "lacking" painted a grim picture. It was a bureaucratic, sterile way of describing the destruction of his life. He was not a partner, a husband, or a loved one; he was a line item, a deficit that needed to be rectified or eliminated.

"But… this is our home," he pleaded, his voice thick with desperation. "We built this together. Remember how excited we were when we found this place? You said it was perfect for us." The memories, once a source of comfort, now felt like cruel taunts. Amina sighed, a sound of deep weariness, but it lacked genuine sorrow. "That was before, Kayode. Before I understood the true cost of living here. Before I realised that dreams don't pay the bills. And frankly, Kayode, I'm beginning to suspect that your capacity for dreaming far outweighs your capacity to provide."

He stood there, frozen, as the enormity of her words washed over him. The man who had left his homeland with hope in his heart, the man who had endured hardship and loneliness for the promise of a better future, now faced the very real prospect of homelessness in a land that had once seemed so full of promise. And the person who held the power to save him, to offer him shelter and security, was the one person who threatened to cast him out into the cold.

"So, what do you want me to do?" he asked, his voice hollow. "Go out there and find another job? Do you think they're lining up for me? I'm a foreigner, Amina. I don't have the qualifications or the network. This is the best I can do." He felt a surge of anger, but a crushing sense of despair quickly drowned it out.

"That's not my problem, Kayode," she said, her voice devoid of emotion. "I need a partner who contributes—a partner who can provide financial security. If you cannot be that partner, I will have to find someone who can. Until you can demonstrate that you can meet your obligations, perhaps you need to consider the consequences."

The consequences. The word hung heavy in the air. Not just financial consequences, but existential ones. The fear of being alone, adrift, without a home, in a foreign country, had haunted his every waking moment since he'd arrived. And Amina, his Amina, was holding that fear over his head.

He looked at her, the woman he had loved, the woman he had trusted implicitly. He saw not the Amina who had held his hand tightly on their wedding day, but a stranger, a woman hardened by the relentless demands of their new life, a woman willing to sacrifice their shared past and future on the altar of financial necessity.

"So, you're saying," he began, the words catching in his throat, "that if I don't have the money… you'll put me out? You'll make me homeless?"

Amina finally looked away, her gaze fixed on the rain-streaked windowpane. Her silence was the answer he dreaded. It was an admission, a confirmation of his deepest fears. The partnership, the shared journey they had embarked upon, had unravelled so completely that it had left him exposed, vulnerable, and facing the terrifying prospect of losing everything. The threats of eviction, once a distant, unthinkable possibility, had become a stark, chilling reality, manipulated by the very person who was supposed to be his sanctuary. He felt a profound sense of betrayal, a sickening realisation that the woman he had followed across the ocean was now the one threatening to cast him adrift.

THE CHILDREN IN THE CROSS FIRE

The thick, suffocating silence that had descended on their small flat was beginning to permeate every corner, not just the space between Kayode and Amina, but the very air the children breathed. It was a silence with no peace in it, only the sharp, brittle edges of unspoken resentments and simmering discord. Maya, barely ten years old, with her wide, inquisitive eyes that missed nothing, was the first to notice. She often trailed behind her mother, her small hand reaching out, only to be met with a distant, preoccupied nod. Her usual giggles, which filled their dwelling as music played, were becoming rarer, replaced by a watchful stillness.

Kofi tried to maintain a semblance of normalcy. He'd retreat to his room to continue building his imaginary superhero, which he had yet to complete. His imaginary superheroes, however, were no match for the looming shadows of his parents' unhappiness. The raised voices, though often hushed when the children were near, carried through the thin walls like distant thunder. He'd pause mid-construction, his small hands faltering as he strained to decipher the tone of the hushed arguments that punctuated their evenings. He'd learned to become exceptionally quiet during these times, a skill he was beginning to develop for self-preservation.

One evening, Amina had been on the phone, her voice tight with frustration. Kayode had entered the room, and though they'd quickly lowered their voices, the tension was a wave that washed over the children. Maya, who had been meticulously arranging her dolls on the rug, froze. Her head tilted, her gaze fixed on the doorway as if anticipating a blow. Kofi dropped his crayon. It rolled away, unnoticed, as he too turned his attention to the escalating, though muffled, exchange between his parents.

"It's just… It's not fair, Kayode," Amina's voice, though low, vibrated with an anger Maya had never heard before. "Every time I try to explain, you just… You shut down or get defensive. And I'm the one left trying to hold everything together."
Kayode's reply was a low murmur, a defensive rumble that only seemed to inflame her further. "Hold everything together? What do you think I'm doing, Amina? Do you think I enjoy this? Do you think I don't see how tired you are? But what am I supposed to do? There's only so much one person can do."

Maya's lower lip trembled. She looked at Kofi, her eyes wide with fear that mirrored his own. He offered her a small, reassuring smile, but it didn't reach his eyes. He reached out and squeezed her hand, a silent pact of solidarity. They were an island, adrift in a sea of their parents' growing discontent.

The arguments weren’t always loud. Often, they were silent wars waged through strained silences, averted gazes, and the clatter of dishes washed with unnecessary force. Amina would sometimes retreat into a frigid stillness, her face a mask of quiet despair, while Kayode would pace the small living room, his shoulders hunched as if carrying an unbearable weight. The children learned to read these moods and to navigate the shifting emotional landscape of their home with caution born of necessity.

Their playtime, once marked by vibrant imagination and joyful abandon, became increasingly punctuated by these atmospheric shifts. A game of chase in the living room might be abruptly halted if the tension between the adults became too much to bear. Maya would often retreat to a corner, hugging her knees to her chest, her bright curiosity dulled by a pervasive sense of unease. Kofi, in his bravado, would sometimes try to intervene, a tiny diplomat in a war he didn't understand.

"Mum, Dad, why are you sad?" he’d ask, his small voice a fragile bridge between their warring factions. He’d try to offer them his drawings, hoping to inject a splash of colour into their grey world. He’d try to engage them in games, tugging at their sleeves, but his innocent attempts to recapture their attention were often met with distracted smiles or a weary sigh.

"It’s okay, Kofi," Amina would say, forcing a brightness into her tone that didn’t reach her eyes. "Mummy is just… tired."

"Daddy is just thinking," Kayode would add, his gaze fixed on some distant point beyond the window, his voice laced with a weariness that seemed to seep into the very fabric of their lives.

But the children weren't fooled. They sensed the undercurrents, the unspoken words that hung heavy in the air. They saw their mother's shoulders sag when she thought no one was looking, and they noticed their father's smiles were becoming increasingly rare and fleeting. They heard the silent cries from their parents' bedroom late at night, sounds that sent shivers of anxiety down their own small spines.

Maya began to internalise the conflict. She had trouble sleeping, waking in the dark with a racing heart, convinced she had heard shouting, even when the house was silent. Her appetite waned, and her teachers at school noticed she was quieter and less engaged than before. She'd often sit alone during playtime, tracing patterns on the classroom floor, her mind miles away. One afternoon, her teacher gently inquired whether everything was all right at home. Aisha, caught off guard by the kindness, shrugged, her eyes welling with unshed tears. She couldn't articulate the fear and confusion, so she remained silent, a small vessel of unspoken anxieties.

Kofi, ever the protector of his older sister, tried to shield her from the worst of it. He'd create elaborate stories for her, spinning tales of brave knights and magical lands where problems didn't exist, where parents always smiled and loved each other. He'd hold her close when the tension in the flat became unbearable, whispering reassurances he didn't entirely believe. But even his childish fantasies and optimism were beginning to fray. The constant exposure to his parents' unhappiness was casting a long shadow over his own burgeoning sense of security.

He developed a habit of hiding. When raised voices began, he'd slip into the small wardrobe in their bedroom, pulling the door almost shut, leaving only a sliver of light. He'd curl up among the clothes, the familiar scent of his parents' laundry brought him some comfort. He'd try to understand what they were arguing about, piecing together fragments of sentences, the angry accusations, the defensive replies. He'd hear words like "money," "bills," "future," words that held a heavy, abstract significance for him, yet he understood their power to inflict pain.

One evening, Amina and Kayode were having one of their hushed yet intensely charged arguments in the kitchen. Kofi, sensing the familiar prelude, had already retreated to his hiding place. Maya, however, was in the living room, playing with a new teddy bear they had received as a gift. The teddy bear, dressed in brown trousers and a white shirt, suddenly became the focus of Maya's unease. She clutched it tightly, burying her face in its soft fabric as the angry murmurs from the kitchen grew louder.

Suddenly, Amina's voice rose, sharper than usual. "I cannot do this anymore, Kayode!" "You simply overestimated yourself, and I cannot keep pretending everything is fine when it's not". "We are drowning!" "I don't feel anything for you right now, Kayode, so please leave me alone".

Kayode was stunned, as though he had been hit by 100 volts of electricity. He was clearly confused by what he had just heard. The discussion concerned his planned visit to the bank. Where did all this come from, he thought to himself, or was this his worst fears unfolding before his eyes? Kayode felt betrayed by the person he had hoped would stand with him through his difficult times. Rumbling with frustration, Kayode stared at Amina, his voice cracking. He stammered, "What are you talking about?" "Is this now about me?" "What do you want me to do, Amina? I'm trying!".

Maya, startled by the increased volume, dropped her doll. It landed with a soft thud on the rug. She stared at it for a moment, then looked towards the kitchen, her eyes wide with fear. Kofi, from his hiding place, heard his sister's cry. A surge of protective instinct, more substantial than his fear, propelled him from the wardrobe. He ran into the living room, his small face etched with worry. "Maya, it's okay," he whispered, his voice trembling. He knelt beside her, putting an arm around her shoulders. "Don't listen to them," he added.

The sound of his voice and his sister's distress cut through the argument. Kayode and Amina fell silent. A moment later, Kayode appeared in the doorway, his face a mask of exhaustion and something like shame. Amina followed, her expression hard, but her eyes held a flicker of something unreadable – perhaps regret, perhaps resignation.

They saw their children, huddled together, a picture of innocent vulnerability caught in the crossfire of their parents' struggles. For a fleeting instant, the anger drained from their faces, replaced by a shared, silent acknowledgement of the damage they were inflicting.

"Come on, you two," Kayode said, his voice softer now, gentler. "It's late. Time for bed."

Kofi, still holding Aisha, looked up at his father. "Will you read us a story, Dad?" he asked, his voice small yet hopeful.

Kayode hesitated, glancing at Amina. She gave a nearly imperceptible nod, her gaze averted. "Yes, son," he said, his tone faintly weary but with a hint of warmth returning. "I'll read you a story."

As they settled into their parents' bed, a rare moment of shared intimacy, Kayode opened a worn book of fairy tales. He read in a low, steady voice, his words a balm against the anxieties that had plagued the household. Maya snuggled close to him, her fear slowly receding, replaced by the comforting rhythm of his voice. Kofi lay beside them, his eyes drooping, the stories a reprieve from the encroaching shadows.

But even as the fairy tales offered a fleeting escape, the children knew, with a child's natural understanding, that the real story unfolding in their lives was far more complex and far less magical. They were migrants in a new land, their parents' dreams of a better life strained by financial pressures and unspoken fears. Amid this struggle, their innocence was tested, their resilience forged in the crucible of their parents' unravelling partnership. The colourful posters of London and the glossy brochures promising opportunity mocked them from their bedroom walls.

This new life, they were beginning to understand, was not a fairy tale but a delicate, often frightening balancing act. They were children in the crossfire, learning to navigate a world that was proving far more complicated and less forgiving than they had ever imagined. The constant tension, the hushed arguments, and the sadness that hung in the air were shaping them, leaving an indelible mark on their young lives, a testament to the profound impact of parental conflict on the most innocent of hearts. They were, in essence, immigrants of a different sort, not just to a new country but to a landscape of adult sorrow they were too young to comprehend fully yet too old to ignore.

CULTURAL MISINTERPRETATION

The knot in his stomach tightened with each passing day, a physical manifestation of the growing rift between them. Kayode found himself replaying their conversations, dissecting Amina's tone, her words, the very way she held herself when they spoke. He'd married a woman who, back home, had been the epitome of quiet grace, who found joy in nurturing their home and their children, and who seemed content with the rhythm of their established life. But here, in the clamour of London, she was transforming, her edges sharpening, her gaze often fixed on some distant horizon he couldn't quite see. He thought of it as a transformation, a shedding of old skins. But was she seeing it the same way? Or had she put a limit on his capacity? He felt betrayed by the deviation from the unspoken promises he thought they had both made.

He remembered their early days, a whirlwind of shared dreams and hopeful whispers. Amina had been excited, yes, but her excitement had been tinged with a familiar sense of duty and a quiet acceptance of their roles. She'd spoken of making their new house a home, of creating a haven for their children, and of supporting him as he navigated the unfamiliar landscape of British work culture. He'd interpreted these words as a partnership, a team effort in which each brought their strengths to the table. He, the provider, the breadwinner, was venturing into the unknown to secure their future. She, the homemaker, the anchor, ensured their family remained grounded and cared for. It seemed a natural division of labour, one he had seen modelled by countless families back home, a time-tested arrangement that ensured stability and clarity.

But here, in this bustling, anonymous city, the lines were blurring, not just for him but more acutely for her. He'd noticed it subtly at first. The way she'd linger over newspaper articles about women's rights, the casual mentions of female colleagues who were climbing corporate ladders, the way she'd started to ask more pointed questions about his earnings, not just how much was left after bills, but what it meant, what it could mean. He'd brushed it off as the natural consequence of being exposed to a more progressive society. He'd seen it as a positive development, a blossoming of her own aspirations. He'd even encouraged it, telling her, "This is England, Amina. Here, you can be anything you want to be." He'd meant it as a liberator, an empowerment.

Now he wondered whether his encouragement had been a careless seed sown in soil already too fertile with unspoken resentments. He'd assumed their financial contributions were clearly defined:

his salary, her careful management of their household budget. But Amina, he was beginning to understand, might have been looking at their situation through a different lens, shaped by the relentless pressures of this new environment. The cost of living was astronomical, a constant worry that hung heavy in the air. Every trip to the supermarket was a strategic manoeuvre, every bill that arrived a small victory or a crushing defeat. He saw her strain, her worry lines deepening, and he tried to reassure her, telling her he was working hard and that things would improve.

What he hadn't grasped was the deep-seated cultural imperative that might have been driving her. In their homeland, a man's worth was intrinsically tied to his ability to provide for and protect his family from financial hardship. A woman's role, while often involving contributing to the household, was fundamentally rooted in the domestic sphere. Seeing her husband struggle, feeling the pinch of poverty, was not just a personal hardship; it was a reflection on his capability and a source of communal shame. Perhaps, in her heart, Amina had expected him to be the unwavering bedrock, the man who could weather any storm without visible strain. And when he, too, showed signs of fatigue and stress, it wasn't just his burden she was witnessing but a perceived failure of the very foundation of their lives.

He'd tried to involve her in the financial discussions to be transparent about their struggles. He'd hoped that by sharing the burden, they could lighten it. He'd explained the challenges of the British tax system, the complexities of getting established, and the long hours he was putting in. He'd presented it as a shared challenge, a united front against adversity. But he now suspected that his overtures towards shared financial planning had been misinterpreted, not as an invitation to collaborate but as an admission of his own inadequacy. Her quiet nods during these discussions, he now saw, might not have been signs of understanding but a dawning disappointment. She might have been waiting for him to fix it, not to discuss how it was broken.

The pressure to conform and succeed was immense. They were not just individuals; they were representatives of their families, their communities, and their nation. Every misstep, every setback, felt amplified, scrutinised by an invisible audience. Amina, he realised, was also navigating the complex web of societal expectations for women in this new, seemingly liberated yet intensely competitive world. She saw other women, not just British women but also immigrant women, striving, achieving, and contributing financially. She heard the casual conversations, the subtle bragging about pay cheque, and the shared anxieties about childcare costs and career progression. And she, who had always been so proud, so determined, was being pulled by these new currents.

He remembered a particular evening, a few months ago, when they'd had a minor disagreement about a new washing machine. His initial thought had been to hold off, to save money. But Amina had been insistent, her voice laced with an urgency he hadn't heard before. "Kayode," she'd said, her eyes pleading, "think of the children. Please think of how much time I spend washing. If I had more time, I could look for something. Something to help." He'd seen it then as a desire to contribute, to ease her workload. He'd agreed, albeit with a sigh, and they'd bought the machine. Now he wondered if her "something to help" had been a coded plea for financial independence, a desire to be more than just the manager of their household expenses.

The partnership he envisioned was one of mutual support within their established roles, a comfortable symbiosis. The partnership Amina, he now suspected, was craving, or perhaps even demanding, was one of equal footing, shared ambition, and a more tangible contribution to their financial well-being. His efforts to be an involved husband and father, to share the domestic load when he could, were perhaps seen not as a sign of his love and commitment but as an indication that he wasn't fulfilling his primary role as the sole provider. His attempts to be a modern man, to share the burdens he perceived, were inadvertently undermining the traditional expectations she might still have held, or those the new environment was subtly reinforcing.

The weight of it all was crushing him. He felt like a failure, not just in his own eyes but in hers too, despite her silence. He'd come to England with a head full of dreams, not just for himself but for his family. He'd envisioned a life where they all thrived, where Amina could pursue her quiet passions, and where the children would have opportunities, he'd never had. He'd seen their journey as a grand adventure, a testament to their strength and resilience. But somewhere along the way, the adventure had become a battlefield, and he was losing his footing, unable to navigate the shifting terrain.

He stared at Amina across the dinner table, her face illuminated by the harsh overhead light. She was meticulously cutting her food, her movements precise, almost mechanical. He wanted to reach out, to touch her hand, to break through the invisible barrier that had risen between them. But what would he say? "Amina, I thought we were a team, but I don't think we're playing the same game?" "Amina, I'm sorry if my attempts to be a modern husband have made you think I'm not a traditional man?" The words felt clumsy, inadequate, a poor reflection of the complex emotions churning within him.

He now understood that cultural expectations were not static, especially when transplanted to new soil. The pressures of migration amplified everything. The constant struggle for financial security, the need to prove oneself in a competitive society, the yearning for the familiar comforts of home while striving for the promise of the new – it was a potent cocktail that could twist even the most well-intentioned dynamics.

He had arrived with his own deeply ingrained cultural lens, expecting a certain harmony, a familiar dance. Amina, too, had brought her own, perhaps even more deeply entrenched, expectations, shaped by years of tradition and the unspoken contract of marriage. In the crucible of their new life, these lenses had begun to warp, to distort, creating a fundamental miscommunication that was now threatening to tear them apart. He had offered what he believed was partnership; she, he suspected, had been seeking something else entirely, something that his efforts, ironically, had failed to provide. The unravelling had begun, not with a bang but with a whisper of misunderstanding, a quiet erosion of shared vision.

ISOLATION AND THE LACK OF SUPPORT

The silence in their small flat had become a tangible presence, a suffocating blanket pressing down on Kayode's chest. It wasn't just the absence of sound, but the lack of shared dialogue, the emptiness of where their conversations used to be. Amina, once his closest confidant, the one person he could unburden himself to, had retreated behind a wall of quiet resignation. Her days were a meticulous choreography of domestic tasks, her nights a restless oblivion punctuated by the hum of the city outside their window. This city felt increasingly alien with each passing day. He longed to speak to her, to bridge the widening gap, but the words always caught in his throat, choked by a growing sense of futility. What could he say? He felt lost. Had the grand adventure of building a new life in England become a relentless, lonely struggle? Were the dreams they had nurtured back home now distant, taunting mirages?

He found himself walking the familiar routes to work; the pavements and red-brick buildings were a stark contrast to the vibrant chaos of Lagos. Each step took him further into his own isolation. Back home, even in times of hardship, there had been a community, a network of family and friends who formed an invisible safety net.

A word with his elder brother, a shared laugh with his trusted neighbours, a comforting visit to his mother's. These were the anchors that had always kept him grounded. Now, those connections were fractured by continents and time zones. A WhatsApp call felt inadequate. He'd tried to explain his predicament, the subtle pressures and anxieties, but the descriptions felt hollow, stripped of the emotional weight they carried for him. He'd hear a sympathetic hum on the other end, a well-meaning boredom, but it was like trying to describe the taste of salt to someone who had only ever known freshwater. The gulf was too vast, the context too different.

The initial excitement of their relocation, the thrill of possibility that had pulsed through them upon arrival, had long since evaporated, leaving a residue of weariness. He remembered their arrival, the optimistic pronouncements about a brighter future, the shared vision of prosperity and opportunity. Amina had been brave, her hand clasped tightly in his as they navigated unfamiliar airports and the bewildering bureaucracy. He had felt a surge of pride and fierce protectiveness, believing he was leading them towards a better life. But now the weight of that responsibility felt crushing.

The dreams of a spacious home, educational opportunities for their children that surpassed anything available back home, and a comfortable retirement – these were no longer distant beacons of hope but heavy burdens that threatened to drag them under. The city, which had promised so much, now felt like a relentless adversary, a cold, indifferent entity that demanded constant struggle and offered little in return.

He would sit in the dimly lit office, the fluorescent lights casting a pale, sterile glow, and trace the lines of his worn hands. They were the hands of a man who had worked hard his entire life, hands that had built, hands that had provided. But here, they felt clumsy, inadequate. The skills he had honed over years of experience in his homeland seemed to hold less currency in this new market. He'd had to adapt, to learn new systems and new ways of working, often for lower pay and with less recognition than he was accustomed to. Each day was a subtle erosion of his confidence, a chipping away at the man he knew himself to be. He was a provider, yes, but the provision felt uncertain. The growing fear of not being able to sustain them and of failing to meet the unspoken expectations that had accompanied him across the sea was a constant companion.

Evenings were the hardest. The flat, meant to be their sanctuary, felt more like a cage. He'd watch Amina move through the rooms, her silence a more profound commentary than any spoken words. He remembered their old home, the vibrant sounds of neighbours greeting each other, the laughter of children playing in the street, and the aroma of familiar cooking wafting from open windows. That sense of connection, of belonging, was a vital nutrient, one he hadn't realised he'd been so dependent on. Here, the neighbours were strangers, their lives as compartmentalised as their terraced houses.

He tried, in his own way, to connect. He'd bring home small tokens, a bar of chocolate, a new book he thought Amina might enjoy. He'd ask about her day, his voice laced with a forced cheerfulness he didn't feel. But her responses were brief, her eyes often distant, as if she were looking through him at something far beyond the confines of their shared reality.

He longed for the easy intimacy they once shared, the comfortable silences punctuated by shared understanding. Now every silence felt heavy with unspoken words, with a growing distance that was becoming an unbridgeable gulf. He was a stranger in his own home, floating in a sea of his own making, and the loneliness was a physical hurt, a hollow space in his soul that no amount of external success could ever fill. The dream of England, once so bright, was beginning to cast long, dark shadows. He was no longer simply a man striving for a better future; he was a man desperately trying not to lose himself in the process. The foundations of his life, both external and internal, felt as if they were beginning to crumble, and he stood alone, watching it happen.

CHAPTER 5

ECHOS FROM OTHER HOMES

THE UNVAILING OF SHARED BURDEN

The weight of Kayode's isolation, the sense of being an outlier in his own struggle, began to lift, not through a sudden revelation or a dramatic shift in his circumstances, but through the quiet, often hesitant sharing of words. It happened in the hushed corners of community centres, during brief encounters at the local church after Sunday services, or over hurried cups of tea in the cramped kitchens of friends' flats. These were spaces where the veneer of success, the carefully constructed façade of 'making it' in the UK, cracked momentarily.

He had initially sought out these men, his fellow citizens, with a hesitant hope that they might offer a different perspective, perhaps a practical solution, or at least a sympathetic ear. He gravitated towards those whose journeys mirrored his own, men who had arrived with similar aspirations, who spoke with the same familiar cadence of Lagos and Ibadan. He'd approach them hesitantly, a cautious probe into the unspoken realities that lay beneath the surface. "How are things, brother?" he'd ask, the question carrying a weight far beyond its casual intent. And then, often, a sigh, a subtle shift in posture, a glance that spoke volumes before any words were uttered.

It began with small admissions. "This weather," one man, a software engineer named Bola, confessed one rainy afternoon, his voice barely above a whisper, "it's enough to drive a man mad, you know? Makes everything feel damp, inside and out." Another, an accountant called Dele, nodded in agreement, adding, "And the loneliness. It hits you when you least expect it. You think you're strong, but this place tests you."

These were surface-level complaints, readily acknowledged, but they were the thin end of the wedge. The honest confessions, the ones that resonated deep within Kayode's weary soul, came later, often after a few more meetings, a growing sense of trust, and a shared understanding that they were all treading water in unfamiliar currents.

One evening, gathered in the back room of a small Nigerian restaurant, the aroma of jollof rice thick in the air, the conversation took a more intimate turn. They were a group of about six men, all professionals, all in their late thirties or early forties, all with families. The usual pleasantries had been exchanged, the football scores dissected, and the latest political gossip from home indulged in. Then there was quiet. It was Tunde, a man Kayode had only recently met, who broke the silence. He spoke of his wife, Funmi, with a mixture of frustration and bewilderment.

"She's… she's changed, Kayode," Tunde admitted, his gaze fixed on his hands, clasped tightly on the table. "Before we came, she was so excited, so supportive. We dreamed together. Now? It's as if she's taken on a new role. She keeps her money and budgets mine for home expenses. And the demands are constant. 'We need this,' 'We need that.' It's always about what we don't have, what we should be buying. And the tone, Kayode. The tone is different." He looked up, his eyes meeting Kayode's with a flicker of desperate recognition. "It's as if she's forgotten where we came from, what we sacrificed."

Kayode felt a jolt, a startling recognition that sent a shiver down his spine. This was not an isolated incident. This was a pattern. Bola, who had initially spoken of the weather and loneliness, now cut in. "You're not alone, Tunde. My wife has become very focused on the material. I work two jobs, Kayode. Two. And still, it's never enough. I come home exhausted, and the first thing I hear is, 'Did you get it? Did you bring it?' It's not just about providing anymore; it's about acquisition. And if I can't, if I say we must wait, then the arguments. The ultimatums." He shook his head, a weary gesture of disbelief. "She says if I don't provide, she'll have to find someone who can. Can you imagine? After all these years, after everything we've been through?"

The words hung in the air, heavy with shared pain and a dawning, unsettling truth. Dele nodded slowly. "My wife sees what other women have, what they post on social media. The holidays, the designer clothes. And she starts comparing. She doesn't understand the sheer effort it takes to earn that here. She thinks it's just easier. She's always wanted a bigger house, a car that's too expensive for us right now. And when I try to explain, to be rational, she tells me I'm not man enough, that I'm holding her back."

Kayode listened, his heart a confusing mix of validation and dread. For so long, he had believed that his own marital struggles were a unique burden, a personal failing, or perhaps a consequence of his own inadequacy in this new land. He had carried the shame of

Amina's increasing distance, her quiet discontent, her subtle criticisms, as a personal cross. He had replayed countless conversations in his mind, dissecting his own words, searching for the precise moment he had gone wrong, the subtle misstep that had led to this growing gap between them.

But here, in this small, fragrant room, surrounded by men who shared his heritage, his language, and now, it seemed, his intimate marital woes, he saw a reflection of his own reality. It wasn't just him. It wasn't just Amina. It was a phenomenon, a tide of marital strain that seemed to be sweeping through their community in the UK. The sacrifices they had made, the dreams they had chased, the very reasons they had left their homeland, seemed to be breeding a new kind of discontent, a perverse twist of fate where the pursuit of a better life was inadvertently fracturing the foundations of their homes.

The women, they surmised, were under immense pressure too. They had left behind their own networks, their mothers, their sisters, their familiar support systems. They were often isolated, facing the same challenges of a new culture, a new climate, and the relentless demands of raising children in an unfamiliar environment. Perhaps, some suggested, the financial control and the insistent demands were a way for them to exert some power in a world where they often felt disempowered. Perhaps it was a desperate attempt to grasp at the tangible symbols of success that they believed were their due, a way to compensate for the emotional and social deprivations they experienced.

"It's the 'grass is greener' syndrome, but amplified," Bola said, churning the last of his drink. "They see the perceived ease of life here, the abundance of goods, and they forget the cost. They forget the sweat and the tears. They start to feel entitled, and when we, their husbands, can't immediately provide what they demand, they lash out. They feel betrayed, I think. Betrayed by us, by England, by the whole idea of this move."

Tunde sighed, a sound of profound weariness. "And we, we are caught in the middle. We carry the weight of providing for the family, of navigating this new system, and of trying to maintain our dignity and sense of self. And then we come home to this pressure. It drains you. It makes you question everything. Was it worth it? Did we make the right decision?"

The conversation continued, a slow, painful unravelling of shared experiences. They spoke of wives who issued ultimatums: "If you can't buy a house, then I'm going back home." Or, "My friends all own their homes. If you cared about your family, you'd care about our comfort and convenience." The subtle jabs, the constant comparisons, and the withdrawal of affection were all weapons utilised in this new domestic battlefield. It was a stark contrast to the communal spirit they had known back home, where neighbours helped neighbours, and families leaned on each other for support. Here, in the perceived land of opportunity, they found themselves increasingly alone, not just in their external struggles, but in their personal lives, with their own wives becoming estranged figures, demanding, condemning and dissatisfied.

Kayode felt a strange sense of relief, a dark comfort in knowing he was not alone. But it was brief. The validation was tinged with deep unease. The problem was not individual; it was systemic, woven into the fabric of their immigrant experience in this new land. For many, the dream of prosperity had become a source of marital discord, a breeding ground for resentment and unmet expectations. The very pursuit of a better future seemed to be eroding the bonds of the present.

He looked around at the faces of the men in the room. He saw the same exhaustion, the same bewilderment, the same quiet desperation he felt within himself. They were strong, capable men, who had built lives and careers in their homeland. But here, in England, they were being tested in ways they had never anticipated, their resilience pushed to its breaking point, not just by the challenges of a new country but by the silent, growing disaffection of the women they loved. These women were supposed to be their partners in this grand, daunting adventure. The shared burden was heavy, a collective weight that pressed down on them, a stark reminder that the echoes from their former homes were not just about nostalgia but about the profound shifts occurring at the core of their families on this foreign soil.

This collective revelation was both a balm and a poison. It was a balm because it dispelled the suspicion that he was uniquely flawed, that his marriage was a singular casualty of his ambition. The fact that so many men, men he respected, men who seemed to have their lives together from the outside, were grappling with strangely similar situations offered a strange, dark comfort. It was as if a secret society, born of shared hardship and unspoken marital

grievances, had opened its doors to him. He wasn't an anomaly; he was part of a collective experience, a shared narrative of familial strain in the diaspora.
However, the poison lay in the sheer scale of the disconcerting realisation that the dream of a better life, the very impetus for their journey, was actively sowing seeds of discord within their homes. The narrative they had sold to themselves and to their wives had been one of aspiration, progress, and a superior future. Now that narrative seemed to be unravelling, replaced by one of unmet desires, financial pressures, and a growing rift in understanding.

The women, it emerged from these hushed conversations, were often the first to feel the pinch of the unfamiliar reality. They had left behind their established social circles, the easy camaraderie of neighbourhood aunties and cousins, and the comforting rhythm of familiar markets. In their place, they found a new, often sterile environment, where neighbours were polite but distant, and the vibrant quality of community life was replaced by isolation within the uniformity of terraced houses and shaped lawns.

One of the men, a doctor named Emeka, his voice drowning in suppressed anger, recounted a recent argument with his wife. "She says she has stopped contributing to household expenses because it is the man's responsibility to take care of his family and that she has done her part in carrying the children in her womb." I told her, 'My dear, any woman can be a mother, but a wife and partner goes beyond just giving birth to children".

All this because I said, "we should manage with the only car we have for now and that the money we're saving should go to our children's education and a down payment for a house." You know what she said? She said, 'Are you ashamed of me? Do you want me to look like a beggar when I go to the school gates?' A beggar! I, who worked day and night to get her here, to give her the life she wanted. And she uses words like that." He ran a hand over his face, his exhaustion palpable. "It's like they've forgotten the struggle. They see the end product, the perceived ease, and they forget the journey. They forget the sacrifices we both made, but they only seem to remember their own discomforts."

Others echoed this sentiment. The women, thrust into a world where consumerism was aggressively marketed and societal status was often measured by material possessions, began to internalise these new values with alarming speed. Social media, they observed, played a significant role, amplifying these desires. Pictures of holidays, designer handbags, and affluent homes flooded their feeds, creating a constant stream of comparison. This, coupled with the absence of their usual support networks, seemed to foster a sense of isolation and heightened material need.

"My wife used to be so content," said Joseph, a graphic designer. "Back home, she was happy with our life. She understood our limitations. Here, it's different. She sees what other Nigerian women have, whether they arrived before we did or about the same time, and she gets agitated. She says I'm not providing enough, that I'm not ambitious enough. But I am ambitious! I'm working myself to the bone! It's just that the system here isn't as straightforward as it is back home. You can't just leverage your network or reputation in the same way. You have to start from scratch and prove yourself all over again."

The notion of 'proving oneself' was a recurring theme. For the men, the struggle was often external – navigating the job market, adapting to new professional cultures, and facing financial pressures. For their wives, the struggle seemed more internal: a battle against isolation, a yearning for the familiar, and a growing sensitivity to the materialistic charm of their new environment. This difference in their struggles, combined with a lack of open communication, perhaps born of exhaustion, pride, and the sheer difficulty of articulating those real fears, created fertile ground for marital strife.

The dynamic of financial control was particularly unsettling. Many of the men revealed that, over time, their wives had taken over the management of their finances, a shift that often began subtly, with the wife handling household bills. But in many cases, it had escalated into an absolute position of financial authority. "She controls everything," Bola admitted, his voice barely a whisper. "My salary goes into our joint account, and then she decides what I get for transport, for lunch, for anything I need. If I ask for extra, for something personal, I have to justify it, plead my case. It isn't very comfortable. I'm a grown man, a provider, and I have to account for every penny to my own wife."

This financial leverage, the men suggested, often translated into emotional leverage. The wives, holding the purse strings, felt empowered, while the husbands felt weakened and controlled. The ultimatums, the constant demands, and the withdrawal of affection – these were tools used to maintain this new power balance. It was a far cry from the partnerships they had envisioned, a shared journey of building a new life together. Instead, it had become a battle for control, recognition, and a sense of security in an uncertain world.

Kayode found himself nodding in silent agreement as the pieces of his fractured reality slotted into place with painful clarity. Amina's quiet insistence that he find a "better job," her subtle criticisms of their modest flat, and her growing disinterest in his well-being began to make sense. It wasn't just his perceived failures; it was a symptom of a broader phenomenon, a collective stress fracturing the foundations of their community.

The conversations in that restaurant, and in other similar gatherings, were not about finding immediate solutions. They were about acknowledging the shared burden and recognising that their individual struggles were part of a larger, more complex picture.

They sought solace in the shared understanding, in the knowledge that they were not alone in their bewilderment and pain. But the unveiling of these shared burdens also brought a profound sense of unease. The dream of England, so carefully constructed and pursued, cast long, dark shadows over their domestic lives, transforming the promised land into a landscape of marital discord and fractured dreams. The echoes from other homes, it turned out, were not just of nostalgia and longing but of the very real challenges reshaping their present and threatening their future.

ANECDOTES OF EXPLOITATION

The weight of unspoken resentments and frustrations, once an isolated burden, had now become a shared one. The men in that fragrant restaurant, and in countless other hushed gatherings, had begun to articulate a truth that had been festering beneath the surface of their immigrant lives. It was a truth that spoke not only of the difficulties of navigating a new country but also of a more insidious form of exploitation at the very heart of their homes. The initial conversations, as Kayode recalled, had focused on the general pressures and the perceived shift in their wives' attitudes. But as trust deepened and the vulnerability of their shared situation became more apparent, the tales that emerged were simpler, more pointed, and undeniably tinged with a sense of betrayal.

One recurring theme was the weaponisation of domestic responsibilities, a tactic that left many men feeling financially trapped and emotionally blackmailed. Joseph, the graphic designer, shared a story about his wife's relentless pursuit of a 'better' neighbourhood, a move that led to a significant increase in their monthly outgoings.

"She'd always talk about the 'good schools' and 'safe streets' in that area," he recounted, his voice laced with a weariness that went beyond mere physical exhaustion. "Then she'd bring up the bills. 'Oh, Joseph, the council tax is so much higher there,' she'd say, with this innocent frown. 'And the electricity, it seems to cost more to heat those bigger houses.' She made it sound like I was personally responsible for the fluctuating energy prices. She would present a list of monthly expenses, meticulously detailing every penny. And at the end, there would always be a note, almost as an afterthought: "So, we'll need an extra £500 this month, won't we?"

It was never a question, you see. It was a statement. And if I hesitated, if I dared to suggest we needed to be more frugal, she'd sigh and say, 'But I don't want the children to suffer, do I? You wouldn't want them to suffer, would you?' It was guilt, pure and simple. She knew I couldn't say no to the children. So I'd find the money. I'd cut back on my own lunches, I'd delay buying new clothes, and I'd even stop going to the barber as often. Anything to meet her 'needs'."

This wasn't just about managing household expenses; it was about a calculated manipulation of their desire to be good providers. Bola, the software engineer, described a similar tactic, in which his wife had taken on the role of 'financial manager' with almost zealous fervour. "At first, I was relieved," Bola admitted, his gaze distant, as if reliving the slow erosion of his autonomy. "I was working those ridiculous hours, two jobs, remember? I barely had time to look at a payslip. So, for her to say, 'Don't worry, darling, I'll handle the bills, I'll make sure everything is paid on time,' it felt like a blessing. But then it shifted. She started asking for more.

'The car insurance has gone up,' she'd say. 'We need to replace the washing machine, it's making a strange noise.' Always a new expense, always a justification that sounded perfectly reasonable on the surface.

Then came the pronouncements. 'We need to contribute more to the joint savings,' she'd say, but the 'more' was always a substantial amount, always beyond what was comfortably affordable without significant sacrifice on my part. I realised later that she was setting aside money for herself, for things she wouldn't tell me about. A secret stash. When I finally confronted her after overhearing her on the phone talking about a 'holiday fund' I knew nothing about, she turned it on me. 'Are you saying I'm not to be trusted?' she asked, her voice trembling with manufactured hurt. 'After all I do for this family? After all, I've given up?' It was a trap. If I pushed, I was the bad guy, the untrusting husband. If I didn't, she continued to control the purse strings, and I continued to feel like a subordinate in my own home.

The appropriation of shared savings was another painful revelation. Emeka, the doctor, spoke with quiet rage about how his wife had unilaterally decided to use a significant portion of their combined savings, accumulated over years of diligent saving back home and early sacrifices in the UK, for a lavish birthday party for their daughter. "We had agreed, very clearly, that that money was for a deposit on a proper house, a family home," Emeka explained, his hands clenched into fists on the table. "It was our security, our future. Then, out of the blue, she announces, 'The children are only young once, Emeka. I want to give our daughter the birthday party she deserves.'

A party, mind you, that involved a bouncy castle, a professional entertainer and a two-tier cake. It was an extravaganza. When I questioned her, I said, 'Where did this money come from? We can't afford this!' She just looked at me, a look of mild surprise on her face, as if I were a dullard. 'From our savings, of course,' she said, as if it were the most natural thing in the world. 'I took it out last week. Don't you want your daughter to be happy?' It was presented as a sacrifice on her part, a mother's love. But it was exploitation. She knew I wouldn't say no to our daughter's happiness, but she also knew the money was crucial to our larger goals. She used our daughter as a shield, a weapon, to get what she wanted.

These stories weren't isolated incidents; they were part of a pattern, a disturbing trend of emotional and financial manipulation that left the men feeling disempowered and exploited within their own domestic spheres. The women, often isolated and struggling to adapt to the new cultural landscape, had found a new form of power, not through open communication or shared decision-making, but through subtle coercion and the exploitation of their husbands' most cherished values – their desire to provide, their love for their children, and their commitment to their families.

The mask of practicality was often the most effective camouflage for these exploitative tactics. Wives would frame their demands not as personal desires but as necessary steps for the family's well-being or social standing. "She'd tell me about other women at the school gates," said Dele, the accountant, his voice heavy with resignation. "Mrs. So-and-so's husband bought, says they are moving their children to a private school next session," she'd say, with a sigh. "We need to invest more in our children's education to get the kind of result that will help them tomorrow."

It wasn't about what she wanted; it was about protecting the children's future and ensuring they weren't 'left behind.' The implication was clear: if I didn't provide these things, I was failing our children. It was a subtle form of blackmail, wrapped in the guise of maternal concern. I ended up taking out a loan to pay for private education, to stop the constant comparisons and the veiled accusations of inadequacy.

The men found themselves in a hole. To voice their concerns or challenge their wives' demands risked being labelled as unloving, unsupportive, or even stingy. The very qualities that had made them attractive partners back home like their generosity, their willingness to sacrifice, their dedication to family, were now being exploited. They had left their homeland seeking a better future, one of prosperity and security. Instead, many found themselves in a situation where their own homes had become arenas of financial struggle and emotional manipulation, where the pursuit of the dream had inadvertently created a new form of subjugation.

They had crossed continents to escape one set of perceived limitations, only to find themselves ensnared by a different, more intimate, form of control. The echoes from their former homes, it seemed, were not just whispers of nostalgia but sharp, sometimes painful, reminders of the unexpected costs of aspiration.

THE ROLE OF EARNING POTENTIAL

The work landscape in Britain, though offering avenues for renewed purpose and financial stability, was also a fertile ground for a subtle, yet profound, shift in marital dynamics. For many, the initial years were a relentless pursuit of any gainful employment, a scramble to establish a foothold. But as time wore on and the unfamiliarity with the UK began to recede, a new reality took shape: the disparity in earning potential between husbands and wives. This phenomenon often carried more weight than mere numbers on a payslip.

It was a common thread that began to emerge in hushed conversations, often over cups of tea or shared meals in the quiet of their own kitchens, or in the more boisterous camaraderie of community gatherings. Wives, who in their home countries might have been homemakers or held positions with less perceived economic contributions, were now finding themselves in roles that were not only financially rewarding but also offered a degree of autonomy that was a stark departure from their previous lives. These weren't necessarily high-flying corporate jobs, though some women did achieve remarkable professional success. More often, they were roles in healthcare, education, administration, or retail, sectors that, while perhaps not yielding exceptional salaries, provided a steady and, significantly, *independent* income.

This newfound financial independence, while a cause for celebration and a testament to their resilience and adaptability, was often accompanied by an increasing sense of empowerment. Suddenly, they possessed the means to contribute significantly, or even unilaterally, to the household budget. This was, in many ways, a positive development, a shared victory.

However, the societal pressures of the UK, the relentless cost of living that seemed to mock their every effort, often cast a long shadow over these victories. The relentless need to keep pace with rising rents, utility bills that appeared to have a life of their own, and the ever-present desire to provide their children with the advantages they felt were essential for success in this new environment began to influence how this financial power was wielded within the marital unit.

For some husbands, the situation was a source of quiet pride. They saw their wives thriving, contributing to the family's well-being, and felt a sense of partnership that was deeply satisfying. But for others, the shift was more complex, often marked by growing unease. The very practicality that enabled their wives to secure these roles could, in some instances, transform into a perceived entitlement or a more assertive approach to financial management. The conversation would no longer be about shared sacrifices, but about expectations, often implicitly or explicitly placed on the husband to continue shouldering most of the domestic expenses.

"She started working as a healthcare assistant," Elias, a former teacher now working in logistics, recounted with a sigh. "It was good work, rewarding, she said. And it was. She brought home a decent wage, enough to cover the groceries and some of the bills. But then, it became an expectation. She'd still mention how much *her* salary was, how it was contributing. But when it came to the rent, of course, another story entirely – the car payments, the children's school trips and extra-curricular activities, it was always, 'Elias, have you sorted that?' It wasn't '*we* need to sort that,' it was always '*you* need to sort that.' Her money, it seemed, was for her, for *her* comfort, for *her* little treats. Mine was for the serious business of keeping a roof over our heads and the children's needs. It felt like a subtle inversion of our roles, where my financial burden increased while her contribution was framed as an act of generosity rather than a shared responsibility."

This perception of a dual standard in financial contribution was a recurring theme. The wives, having secured their own independent income, might find themselves with disposable income that allowed for small luxuries or personal pursuits. This could manifest in anything from regular visits to the beauty salon and body massages to occasional shopping sprees. However, when it came to the larger, non-negotiable expenses of running a household in the UK, the onus often remained, or was subtly shifted back, onto the husband.

"My wife, bless her, she's a brilliant administrator," explained David, who worked long hours in a warehouse. "She found a job in an office, with decent hours and good colleagues. She's always been organised and meticulous. And she uses that organisational skill at home, too.

Lately, it's become strategic. She'll present me with bills, always neatly itemised, of course, and say, 'This is what we owe.' Then she'll add, 'I can cover the electricity this month, but the gas is a bit more. And the internet… It's going up again, isn't it?' It sounds reasonable. But what she doesn't mention is that her 'contribution' to the electricity bill is often less than what she spends on her weekly lunches with friends or the new handbag she 'needed' for work. And then there are the 'spurs' she likes to visit. Weekend trips to London, a few days in Edinburgh with her friend. She frames it as 'needing a break,' 'a bit of me-time.' And I'm happy for her to have that. But when she's away, who's managing the household? Who's making sure the children are fed, that their homework is done, that I'm not completely overwhelmed? It's still me.

When she returns, refreshed and revitalised, the financial conversations begin anew, with her looking at me as if I've been hoarding money. She'll say things like, 'So, have you managed to put anything aside for that new sofa we need? I saw a lovely one online, but it's quite expensive.' The implication is that my money should go towards shared needs, while her money should go towards her personal rejuvenation and exploration. It's a subtle, but very real, shift in the power dynamic."

The appeal of travel and leisure, perhaps less accessible in their home countries, became a tangible benefit of their newfound earning power. For some wives, these "spurs," as David put it, were more than just holidays; they were a lifeline, a way to reconnect with a sense of self that the demanding realities of immigration and domestic life had subsumed. They were also, in some instances, a visible symbol of their independence, a declaration that they were no longer solely defined by their roles as wives and mothers.

However, this newfound freedom often came at the cost of marital equilibrium. Husbands, who might have been accustomed to a more collaborative approach to finances, found themselves grappling with a new set of unspoken rules. The expectation that they would continue to be the primary breadwinners, covering the lion's share of household expenses, while their wives enjoyed the fruits of their independent earnings, fuelled resentment for some.

"It's the holidays that get me," confessed Kwame, a skilled carpenter who now worked in construction. "My wife is a qualified nurse. She works long shifts. She earns well, more than I do now. And I'm proud of her, truly. But every few months, it's a trip.

‘I need to see my sister in Spain,’ or ‘The girls are going to Italy for a short holiday.’ She’ll book it, and then she’ll say, ‘Don’t worry about me, darling, you and the children just enjoy yourselves. I’ll be back in a week.’ And I do. I manage. I take the children to the park, and we have pizza nights. But then she’ll call, and the first thing she’ll ask is, ‘Did you pay the council tax this month?’ or ‘Have you managed to save for the car insurance renewal?’ It’s as if her time away is a separate entity, funded by her earnings, while all the ongoing, mundane, expensive responsibilities of our life here are still implicitly mine to bear. She doesn't seem to grasp that her absence, while a holiday for her, is a period of increased workload and financial management for me. And when she returns, she’s refreshed and relaxed, and I’m just tired. And then the conversation turns to how we can ‘treat ourselves’ next. But it’s always my wallet that seems to be the primary source for these ‘treats.’ It’s a strange sort of imbalance, where the joy and freedom she gains from her work seem to be directly proportional to the burden it places on me to maintain the status quo at home."

The socio-economic underpinnings of these marital conflicts were complex and multi-layered. Pressures from the UK, the cost of maintaining a particular lifestyle, and deeply ingrained societal expectations of gender roles, even as they were being challenged by women's increasing participation in the workforce, all played a part.

For some couples, the shift in earning potential was a catalyst for a more equitable partnership, a renegotiation of roles and responsibilities that benefited everyone. They embraced the opportunity for shared financial planning, mutual support, and a balanced distribution of earnings and domestic duties.

However, for others, the wife's newfound financial independence became a source of unintended friction. It could lead to a subtle or not-so-subtle reassertion of previous norms, in which the husband's role as the primary provider was expected to remain sacrosanct, even as the wife's income grew. The "spurs" and "breaks" abroad, while perhaps well-intentioned as moments of personal respite, could inadvertently highlight differences in their experiences, creating a sense of disconnect and contributing to the feeling that the shared dream of a better life was being pursued on slightly different terms. Earning potential, therefore, was not just about the figures on a payslip; it was about the complex interplay of power, expectation, and evolving marital dynamics in the crucible of a new land.

CHAPTER 6
THE CHILDREN'S DIVERGENT PATH

ALTERATION SHOCK

The children, Maya and Kofi, had been caught in the crossfire of their parents' unspoken anxieties and had now adapted coping mechanisms. For Maya, the elder at thirteen, the move to London was an abrupt, disorienting fall into a world where everything felt amplified.

The bustling streets, the noise of unfamiliar accents, the sheer scale of the city – it was a sensory overload that demanded a swift, decisive response. Unlike her younger brother, whose introspection led him inwards, Maya's reaction was outward, a fierce channelling of her intellect towards academic achievement. She saw the worried frowns that creased her parents' foreheads, the hushed, strained tones of their conversations that seemed to thicken the air in their small flat. She understood, with a child's intuitive grasp, that something was amiss, and she instinctively sought a way to fix it, to mend the invisible tears in their family fabric.

Her school became her sanctuary, a place where the rules were clear, the objectives defined. The Nigerian curriculum, with its emphasis on repetition learning and strict discipline, had equipped her with a solid foundation. Still, the British system offered a different kind of intellectual stimulation, a demand for critical thinking and independent analysis that Maya found both challenging and exhilarating. She devoured textbooks, her small bedroom transformed into a study, piled high with library books and revision notes. The glow of her desk lamp became a familiar beacon in the evenings, illuminating her room as she wrestled with complex equations or delved into Shakespeare's different writing styles.

She saw her grades not merely as marks on a report card, but as tangible proof of her worth, a potential key to unlock a future of stability and security for her family. Each commendation from a teacher, each A grade achieved, was a small victory, a quiet offering at the altar of their collective well-being. She imagined a future where she, armed with a prestigious university degree, could secure a well-paying job that would help alleviate the financial burdens that seemed to weigh so heavily on her parents.

This vision fuelled her relentless drive, pushing her to excel in every subject and to participate in every extracurricular activity that might support her university applications. She joined the debate club, honing her articulate speaking skills, and volunteered at the local library, expanding her knowledge base and demonstrating her commitment to community service. Her determination was a force to reckon with, a bright spark against the encroaching shadows of uncertainty.

Her ambition, however, began to cast a subtle shadow on her relationship with her peers. Maya, respected for her intelligence, was often set apart by her single-minded focus. She usually spent her lunchtimes poring over textbooks, and social gatherings were seen as distractions from her goal. Her classmates, navigating the typical adolescent dramas of friendships and first crushes, found Maya’s unwavering dedication somewhat perplexing. They’d invite her to parties, to go shopping, to hang out, but her polite refusals, always accompanied by a brief explanation of her study schedule, became a regular occurrence. "I have a mock exam next week," she'd say, or "I need to finish this research paper for history." She wasn't unfriendly, but her earnestness and the sheer weight of her self-imposed mission created an invisible barrier.

This intellectual isolation, while seemingly a necessary sacrifice, began to weigh on her. There were moments when she yearned for the carefree laughter of her classmates, for the easy companionship she saw them sharing. But the fear of falling behind, the ingrained understanding of what was at stake, always pulled her back to her books, her unwavering resolve a double-edged sword that both propelled her forward and isolated her from the very generation she was a part of.

Kofi, on the other hand, was like a tree bending under an invisible storm. At ten years old, his vibrant energy, once a constant source of delight to his parents, seemed to be slowly fading. The boisterous boy who had once chased pigeons in the parks of Lagos and initiated impromptu games of football with neighbourhood children now moved through their London flat with a quiet, almost ghostly, presence. The vibrant colours of his imaginary world, once so vivid, had begun to fade.

The constant sound of worry in the house had seeped into his young consciousness, transforming his playful curiosity into a hesitant caution. He observed his parents' strained smiles, the way his mother’s eyes would often dart towards the pile of bills on the kitchen counter, the way his father would sometimes retreat into himself after long workdays, his shoulders slumped with an exhaustion that went beyond physical fatigue. He didn't have Maya's analytical mind to dissect the situation, but he felt the uneasiness in his very bones.

His school now felt like a foreign land. The playground, once a stage for uninhibited joy, now seemed a complex social battlefield. He struggled to understand the fast-paced slang, the intricate social hierarchies, and the unspoken codes of conduct that appeared to govern interactions among his British classmates. His accent, once a point of pride, now felt like a mark of his difference. Children sometimes asked him where he was from; their questions, tinged with curiosity that bordered on interrogation, made him stammer out his answers, wishing he could blend in, be invisible. The easy friendships he had known back home, forged through shared laughter and spontaneous play, seemed elusive here. He found himself gravitating towards the quieter corners of the playground, observing rather than participating, his gaze often fixed on the ground.

His withdrawal manifested itself in his love of solitary pursuits. He rediscovered his passion for drawing, filling sketchbooks with fantastical creatures and elaborate imaginary cities, worlds where he was in control, and the rules were his own. He also became an avid reader, losing himself in tales of knights and dragons, of brave adventurers facing insurmountable odds. Books offered an escape, a reprieve from the anxieties that lay beneath the surface of his young life. He would spend hours with his nose buried in a book, the outside world fading into a distant buzz. His parents, caught in their own struggles, saw his quiet nature as a sign of adjustment, a testament to his resilience. They praised his studiousness and his ability to entertain himself, unaware of the deeper currents of loneliness and apprehension shaping his young world.

Maya, despite her own intense focus, couldn't help but notice the change in her brother. She saw how he would shrink back when addressed and how his eyes often seemed clouded with a sadness too profound for his years. She tried to draw him out, to engage him in conversations about his day, to coax him into playing games with her, but her efforts were often met with shy smiles and mumbled responses. "I'm just reading, Maya," he'd say, or "I'm drawing."

She recognised the echo of her own struggles in his isolation, though her path to coping was vastly different. She understood that his silence wasn't a lack of engagement with the world, but a different kind of engagement, a retreat into the safety of his own imagination. She often felt guilty, a sense that, in her pursuit of individual success, she was not adequately present for her younger brother. She'd try to share snippets of her school day with him, hoping to spark a shared experience, but the gulf between their worlds, her academic ambitions and his growing emotions often felt too wide to bridge easily.

The cultural difference between their Nigerian upbringing and their new British reality was a constant presence in their lives. At home, the familiar rhythms of Nigerian culture remained. Their mother, Amina, despite her own mounting worries, still insisted they speak Yoruba at home and prepared the familiar dishes of their homeland, filling their small flat with the comforting aromas of jollof rice and plantain. These were anchors to their past, vital threads of their identity. Yet outside the sanctuary of their home, they were immersed in a distinctly British world. The language at school was English, the social norms were British, and the cultural references were often entirely alien.

Maya, with her determined intellect, absorbed this new culture with strategic pragmatism, learning to code-switch effortlessly and to navigate both worlds with conscious effort. She understood that fluency in English, coupled with an understanding of British social cues, was essential to her success. She observed her classmates, noting their turns of phrase, mannerisms, and shared cultural touchstones. She meticulously incorporated them into her own interactions, like an anthropologist studying a new tribe.

Kofi, however, struggled more acutely with this duality, particularly with the rapid shifts in language and social expectations. One moment, he was reprimanded by his mother in flowing Yoruba for not finishing his homework; the next, he was asked by his teacher in crisp English to "put his hand up if he understood."

The inherent differences between the communal, social interactions of Nigerian life and the more reserved, individualistic approach prevalent in Britain left him perpetually out of step. He missed the easy physical contact of his homeland, the spontaneous hugs and hand-holding common among children there. Here, people seem to define their personal space. This subtle but significant shift in social etiquette left him feeling disconnected, as if he were constantly misinterpreting social signals. His drawings, once filled with vibrant scenes of Nigerian life, began to feature more solitary figures, often looking out at vast, empty landscapes, a visual representation of his internal experience.

The tension at home, though rarely expressed in outright conflict, was a constant, low-grade fever that affected them both. Maya, in her relentless pursuit of academic excellence, saw her efforts to counteract this tension as a shining beacon of hope that would somehow ease her parents' worries. She was a warrior of the classroom, her ambition her shield and sword against the encroaching gloom. She believed that if she could achieve enough, if she could secure a place at a good university and then a successful career, she could somehow "fix" their financial situation, making their sacrifices worthwhile. This immense, self-imposed pressure often left her exhausted, the weight of her family's hopes resting heavily on her young shoulders. She would sometimes lie awake at night, her mind racing through to-do lists and study plans.

Kofi, on the other hand, absorbed the tension like a sponge. He didn't understand the complexities of their financial struggles. Still, he felt the palpable shift in his parents' demeanour, the weariness in his father's voice, the worry in his mother's eyes, and the way laughter seemed to have become a rarer commodity. He sensed that their happiness was tied to their struggles, and this created a deep-seated anxiety within him. His withdrawal was a form of self-preservation, a way to shield himself from the emotional storm he perceived brewing around him. He sought refuge in his books and drawings, creating a buffer between himself and the often-unsettling realities of his parents' lives.

He longed for the carefree days of their old life, the ease and joy that seemed to have left on the shores of Nigeria. His quietness was not a sign of indifference but a testament to a young soul grappling with a world that felt increasingly precarious and confusing. The divergent paths of Maya and Kofi, one forging ahead with determined ambition, the other retreating into a shell of introspective silence, both responded to the acculturation shock that had rippled through their family, a silent testament to the complex and often painful process of forging a new identity in a new land.

NAVIGATING SCHOOLYARD POLITICS

The buzz of the school bus, a sound so alien to the familiar, chaotic noise of Lagos, was the start of Maya's day in British secondary school life. She sat by the window, the rain-marked glass mirroring a world that still felt, at times, like a dream. Her textbooks, a comforting weight on her lap, were her constant companions. They offered predictability and a clear path from question to answer which was a stark contrast to the unclear, unwritten rules that governed the corridors of her school in Lagos.

Her academic prowess was undeniable. Teachers praised her meticulous notetaking, her insightful contributions to English literature discussions, and her lightning-fast grasp of complex mathematical concepts. Back in Nigeria, her forthrightness in class and her immediate raising of a hand with a confident answer had been seen as a sign of diligence and intelligence. Here, however, it sometimes elicited a different reaction. A raised eyebrow from a classmate, a subtle shift away on a bench, a whispered comment that hung in the air like static. She had once, with the best of intentions, pointed out a factual inaccuracy in a historical explanation given by a substitute teacher. In Lagos, this might have been met with a nod of acknowledgement, perhaps even a gentle correction. Here, the teacher visibly stiffened, and a ripple of unease spread through the classroom. Maya, observing this, felt confused. Was directness a virtue only in specific contexts?

She noticed the unspoken currents that flowed beneath the surface of adolescent interactions. The way certain groups gravitated together, their laughter a shared language Maya hadn't yet fully learned. The subtle cues that signalled inclusion or exclusion – a shared glance, a knowing smile, a whispered secret. In Lagos, friendships were formed in the neighbourhood's communal spaces, built on shared games and open, unfiltered conversations. Here, the social landscape felt more intricate, more guarded. Cliques formed, seemingly from invisible threads of shared experiences, familial connections, or simply a natural magnetic pull.

Maya began to observe. She watched Chloe, a blonde-haired girl, navigate these social waters with confidence. Chloe didn't dominate conversations, but she was always at their centre, her comments light and humorous, her questions open-ended, inviting participation. Maya noticed that Chloe prefaced potentially critical observations with phrases like "I'm not sure if this is right, but..." or "Could it be that...?" It was a softening, a deliberate cushioning of her words. Maya began to experiment, adopting a slightly more tentative tone and softening her direct questions with polite preambles. It felt unnatural, like wearing ill-fitting clothes, but she was determined to find a way to bridge the gap.

She also noticed the subtle ways her background was perceived. Comments about her accent, though often framed as curiosity, sometimes felt like an emphasis on her difference. "Where are you really from?" was a question she'd grown accustomed to, even when she'd already stated she was from Nigeria. There was an assumption that "African" was a monolithic identity, and her specific Nigerian heritage seemed to be a footnote rather than a defining characteristic.

To navigate this, Maya found herself unconsciously downplaying certain aspects of her identity. She might omit mentioning her love for certain Nigerian foods in casual conversation or nod along when a classmate made a generalised observation about "Africa" that felt inaccurate or stereotypical. It wasn't a conscious rejection of her heritage, but a subtle adaptation, a learned behaviour to facilitate smoother social interactions. She learned to code-switch not just in language but in persona. At home, she was Amina's bright, ambitious daughter. At school, she was Maya, the diligent student, striving to be just another face in the crowd, albeit a very intelligent one.

She was acutely aware of the pressure to conform and assimilate. It wasn't just about fitting in socially; it was about securing her academic future, which she saw as linked to her ability to navigate this new environment successfully. Her parents' sacrifices weighed on her, a constant reminder of why she couldn't afford to be an outsider. She'd seen how some immigrant children at school were sometimes subjected to casual teasing or exclusion, and the thought of becoming a target filled her with cold dread. So she studied. She studied British slang from teen magazines she borrowed from the library, practised the inflections of common phrases, and tried to adopt a more laid-back posture, less formal than the one she'd cultivated in Nigeria. It was a complex dance, requiring constant vigilance and a keen eye for detail.

Meanwhile, Kofi's experience in the playground was a different kind of bewildering. At ten, he was at an age when friendships could be both intensely loyal and incredibly erratic. The rough-and-tumble football games that had been a constant in his Lagos life were different here. There was a perceived physicality, a speed, and a set of unwritten rules that seemed to change from one game to the next. He found himself on the periphery, an observer rather than a participant.

The language barrier, while not insurmountable for him in formal lessons, became a significant hurdle in the playground's informal, rapid-fire exchanges. Slang, jokes, and references to popular culture flew over his head like invisible missiles. He would hear bursts of laughter erupt from a group of boys, try to decipher the joke, only to be met with confused stares when he tentatively asked, "What's funny?" The typical response was a shrug or a murmur, "You wouldn't get it," which only deepened his sense of isolation.

He missed the interactions he had known before. In Nigeria, a child might spontaneously join a game already in progress and be welcomed with open arms. Here, there is an implicit vetting process. A new child must prove their worth, skills, and ability to understand the game's intricate dynamics before being fully integrated. Kofi, with his gentler disposition and more reserved nature, found this process daunting. He was less inclined to assert himself, to push his way into a game, and so he often found himself watching from a distance, a solitary figure leaning against the brick wall of the school building.

His drawings became his refuge. He would sketch elaborate scenarios in his notebook, depicting himself as a valiant knight defending a castle or a daring explorer charting unknown territory. In these worlds, he was the hero, in control and respected. He would re-enact the playground battles he experienced during the day in his sketchbook, but with a different outcome – one where he was always the victor, always accepted. He would create characters that mirrored the children he saw but load them with the qualities he admired – bravery, kindness, fairness. He'd sometimes draw himself interacting with these characters, a silent conversation taking place on the page.

He noticed the unspoken social hierarchy: the 'cool kids' who seemed to command others' attention and admiration with effortless ease. There was a subtle, almost imperceptible shift in how children interacted with these individuals, a deference he found perplexing. He saw how minor infractions, such as a misspoken word or a clumsy move during a game, were often overlooked in favour of these favoured few. By contrast, similar missteps by others might prompt immediate mockery. Kofi, with his sensitive soul, felt the injustice keenly but lacked the social capital to challenge it or even fully comprehend it.

His attempts to connect were met with polite indifference or outright dismissal. He would try to show his drawings to other children, hoping to spark a shared interest, but the conversations would rarely last. "That's good," they would say, their eyes already scanning for a more exciting distraction or a more engaging peer. He knew when to retreat before outright rejection.

Maya, despite her own academic pressures, would watch Kofi's quiet retreat with growing unease. She'd see him on the periphery of playground activities, his shoulders slumped, his gaze fixed on the ground. She'd try to draw him out at home, asking about his day and his friends. His answers were usually vague, "fine" and "nothing much." She knew, however, that "nothing much" often meant "too much to explain" or "nothing worth sharing." She'd offer to help him with his homework, play a game of chess, or sit and draw with him, but he'd often politely decline, retreating further into his own world.

One afternoon, she found him alone on a bench at lunchtime, his head buried in a book. She sat beside him, the scent of his well-thumbed pages a familiar comfort. "What are you reading, Kofi?" she asked softly.

He looked up, his eyes wide and a little startled. "It's about a boy who finds a magical map," he whispered, his voice barely audible above the din of the cafeteria.

Maya smiled, a genuine smile that reached her eyes. "That sounds exciting." She paused, then added, "You know, I saw some children playing a new card game at break time. It looked quite fun. They were using a lot of strategy, like in chess." She was subtly trying to bridge the gap, offering him a narrative that might resonate with his interests and connect him to the social world he found so daunting.

Kofi nodded, but his gaze drifted back to the pages of his book. Maya understood. Her methods for coping with and navigating this new world were so different from his. She tackled it head-on, with logic and ambition. He retreated into himself, creating a sanctuary within. She was the seasoned diplomat, learning the intricate protocols of a foreign court. He was the solitary explorer, charting his own hidden territories. Both were strategies for survival, for forging an identity in a land that felt both promising and profoundly alien. For them, the schoolyard was a miniature of their larger journey; in this complex arena, adaptation, resilience, and the quiet longing for belonging played out in a thousand small, unspoken dramas.

BRIDGING TWO WORLDS

The aroma of jollof rice would often waft through the house on a Sunday afternoon. It was a deliberate ritual, a conscious effort to anchor his children to the shores of their homeland. He'd meticulously prepare the dish, the familiar scent of tomatoes, peppers, and spices a comfort to his own soul, a hope that it would be a similar comfort to theirs. He would call out, his voice warm with anticipation, "Children! Come! Your father has made us some real Nigerian jollof!"

Maya, engrossed in her meticulously organised revision notes, would emerge with a polite smile on her lips. “It smells amazing, Dad,” she would say, her tone carefully modulated, a testament to her growing command of subtle social cues. The jollof was a tangible part of her past, delicious. But the present held a more immediate attraction.

Kofi, on the other hand, would pick at the rice, a small smile plastered on his face, murmuring his appreciation. But his eyes would often flick towards the television, where cartoons in BBC-accented English played, or to the worn comic book lying on the coffee table, its pages filled with heroes speaking in a language that felt more natural to him than the Yoruba proverbs his father would sprinkle into his storytelling. The act of eating jollof, while a duty to the family and a nod to his heritage, felt increasingly like a performance, a role he was playing for his father's sake, rather than a genuine expression of his own desires.

He tried, in his own way, to bridge the gap. He once brought some leftover jollof to school as an act of defiance against the tasteless packed lunch. He offered his friend, Liam, "Try this, it's Nigerian!" Liam was a boy with an infectious smile who loved to play football. Liam took a spoonful of Kofi's jollof rice. "It's... spicy," he said, his voice laced with politeness. He hadn't refused it outright, but he hadn't asked for more either. The unspoken judgement and subtle recoil had been a powerful lesson. Kofi retreated. The uneaten portion in his lunchbox now felt like a burden.

His father would introduce them to the rhythm and soul of Nigerian music. He would put on Fela Kuti, his feet tapping to the infectious beat. He would watch his children, hoping to see a spark of recognition, a shared enthusiasm. Maya, ever the dutiful daughter, would nod along, her head swaying in a rhythm that felt more like imitation than an organic response. She would complement the music, "It's very lively, Dad," her words carefully chosen to avoid any hint of negativity. But privately, her playlists featured the popular hits of British pop stars who dominated the school's social sphere. The rhythms of Afrobeat felt distant, almost alien, compared with the immediate, accessible energy of the music her peers listened to.

Kofi often sat with his gaze fixed on the speaker. He had not yet learned to navigate the music's raw emotion. It felt loud and overwhelming, and sometimes he found himself confessing to himself that the sound was annoying. He would much rather listen to the ambient electronic music he discovered online or the soundtracks to the video games he played. These sounds created an atmosphere, a mood, without demanding it. When his father asked him what he thought, he would mumble something about it being "interesting". In his young lexicon, that meant "I don't really get it, and I don't want to offend you."

Kofi sometimes steered the conversation to his own stories, the worlds he conjured in his sketchbooks. He once showed his father a drawing of a spaceship crew, their uniforms emblazoned with symbols he had invented, embarking on a mission to a distant galaxy. His father examined it with a fond smile. "This is very good, Kofi. But do you remember the story of the tortoise who tricked the lions? He was very clever too." The gentle redirection, while well-intentioned, felt like a dismissal of Kofi's creative impulse, a subtle suggestion that his imagined worlds were less valid than those rooted in their shared heritage.

The disconnect wasn't sudden but a slow, almost gradual erosion. It manifested in subtle ways. The slang Maya began to embed in her sentences, with terms like "buzzing," "grand," and "innit," which would earn her approving nods from Chloe and her friends but often elicit a curious look from her father. He would sometimes ask, "What does that mean, Amina?" and Maya, with a practised ease, would translate, often delivered with a slight blush, a subtle apology for the foreignness of it all.

Similarly, Kofi's pronouncements on the latest superhero movie and the intricate plots and character analyses he shared with Liam would often be met with a patient nod from his father. He would try to explain the scenes, but his father's eyes would usually glaze over, his mind perhaps still lingering on the allegories of a different kind of heroism. Kofi learned to moderate his enthusiasm and reserve his passionate critiques for his British friends, who understood and reciprocated them.

He noticed that his father's attempts to connect sometimes felt like an imposition. There were days when he just wanted to be "normal," to fit in without having to navigate the two distinct cultures consciously. He would see his father carefully packing moi-moi into a Tupperware container for his lunch. But then he would see Liam unpacking a neat sandwich and a bag of Haribo sweets, and he would feel envious and silently wish for the same. He would sometimes trade his Nigerian lunch for a friend's crisps and a biscuit. This act left a bitter taste in his mouth, not from the food but from the guilt of disappointing his father and rejecting a part of himself.

Maya, despite her own internal negotiations with identity, was keenly aware of her father's efforts. She saw the earnestness in his eyes when he spoke of Nigeria, and the pride that swelled in his chest when he introduced them to a new Nigerian artist or shared a family anecdote. She loved him deeply and understood the importance of heritage. But her world was expanding, shaped by her environment. Her friendships, her academic aspirations, and her very sense of self were moulded by the British landscape she inhabited daily. She found herself walking a tightrope, trying to honour her past without sacrificing her future, to remain connected to her roots while embracing the opportunities that lay before her.

The Sunday dinners, once vibrant with shared stories and laughter, began to sour. His father would start a story about his own childhood in Lagos, painting pictures of a world that felt increasingly like a fairy tale to his children. He would talk about the freedom of playing in the streets until dusk, the communal spirit of neighbourhood gatherings, and the warmth of an extended family always present. Maya would listen, her mind noting the details, perhaps for a future essay and a deeper understanding of her family's history. Kofi, however, would often fidget, his gaze drifting towards the window, a silent longing for the world outside, one with his friends, his games, his own identity.

"And then," his father would say, his voice resonating with nostalgia, "we would all gather for the naming ceremony. The drumming, the dancing, the feast! It was a time of great joy, a celebration of new life."

Maya would nod, a polite "That sounds wonderful, Daddy" escaping her lips.

Kofi, his mind on the upcoming football match, might mumble, "Yeah, cool."

The words hung in the air, polite acknowledgements of a culture that was slowly becoming a memory. Kofi was trying to build a bridge to ferry them across the divide, but the currents of their new lives were pulling them in a different direction.

He brought them to a new land of opportunity, a place where their potential could flourish. But he had not anticipated how profoundly that land would reshape them, how its very essence would weave itself into the fabric of their beings, creating a new culture in which the threads of their Nigerian heritage, though still present, were becoming intertwined with the vibrant, ever-expanding patterns of British life. He watched them, his heart a mixture of pride and a quiet, persistent ache, as they navigated the complexities of their dual existence, their divergent paths already widening with each passing day. He was a gardener, tending two different species of plant in the same soil, each with its own needs, its own bloom, its own destiny. He could nurture them, provide them with water and light, and they would ultimately grow in their own directions, reaching for their own suns.

THE IMPACT OF PARENTAL CONFLICT

The air in the house, once thick with the comforting aroma of his wife's cooking and the hum of contented family life, had grown thin and brittle, prone to shattering at the slightest discord. His children, so acutely attuned to the shifting atmospheric pressure of their home, responded in ways that tore at his heart. He saw it in Maya's almost frantic pursuit of academic perfection. Her eyes, once bright with youthful curiosity, now often held a distant, determined gleam, her brow perpetually furrowed in concentration. She buried herself in textbooks, her fingers tracing complex formulas and dense prose as if they offered a tangible shield against the invisible tremors of their parents' arguments. Her pristine bedroom, once a haven of teenage clutter, was now an altar to order, her stationery meticulously arranged, her notes colour-coded with an almost obsessive precision.

He knew, with a certainty that chilled him, that her academic achievements, her perfect scores, her burgeoning list of extracurricular accolades, were not solely born of a love of learning. They were a desperate offering, a plea for stability, a misguided attempt to earn a peace that eluded their household. She was trying to be the perfect child, the flawless embodiment of what a good daughter should be, in the hope that her unassailability would somehow insulate her from the corrosive effects of their conflict. He'd watched her stay up late, the lamp in her room casting a solitary glow long after the rest of the house had fallen silent, the rhythmic scratch of her pen a constant, melancholic underscore to the unspoken tension downstairs.

Kofi, on the other hand, had retreated into a labyrinth of quietude. His vibrant energy, once expressed in boisterous laughter and enthusiastic declarations, had dimmed to a barely perceptible flicker. He moved through the house like a ghost, his footsteps soft, his voice often reduced to a murmur. He found solace in the digital realms, the glowing screens of his video games offering an escape from the harsh realities of his home. In these virtual worlds, he could be a hero, a conqueror, a master of his own destiny, unburdened by the emotional turmoil swirling around him. He'd spend hours in his room, the door often closed, a silent barrier between himself and the fractious world outside.

When he did emerge, it was with forced casualness, his eyes darting nervously between his parents, a perpetual caution in his posture. He'd learned to anticipate the storm clouds, to sense the rising tension before it broke, and his primary strategy was to become as small and as invisible as possible. He often ate his meals in silence, his gaze fixed on his plate, his small hands pushing food around the ceramic landscape, a mirror of his own internal stillness. He'd perfected the art of the non-committal nod, the brief, almost inaudible "yes" or "no," anything to avoid engaging in conversations that might draw unwanted attention or, worse, inadvertently exacerbate the fragile peace. His quietness was not contentment but a profound, deeply ingrained fear.

He remembered a particular evening, not long ago, when a minor disagreement over a forgotten chore had escalated into a full-blown shouting match. Maya, engrossed in her homework at the kitchen table, had flinched with each raised voice, her hands flying to cover her ears as if to block out the venomous words. Kofi, who had been sketching in the living room, had vanished. Later, he found him curled up in his bed, a thin blanket pulled tight around him, his small body trembling. He hadn't cried, not outwardly.

Instead, he'd whispered, his voice barely audible, "When will it stop, Papa? When will it just be quiet again?" The raw desperation in his son's voice had been a physical blow, a searing indictment of the environment he had, through his own failings, allowed to take root. The guilt, a familiar companion, had tightened its grip, suffocating him.

He observed, with a heavy heart, that their dreams had become inextricably linked to the elusive concept of parental harmony.

Maya, who had once spoken of becoming a veterinarian, of healing and caring for animals, now spoke with fervent conviction of securing scholarships, attending Oxbridge, and building a future on professional success and financial independence. She understood that her ambition was commendable, a manifestation of her sharp intellect and diligent work ethic. But he also saw the underlying desperation, the unspoken belief that if she achieved enough, if she became indispensable, perhaps her parents would be forced to find a way to coexist, to present a united front. Her future, once a canvas of boundless possibility, was now being painted in the stark colours of necessity, the vibrant hues of childhood whims replaced by the muted tones of adult responsibility, shouldered far too soon.

Kofi's aspirations, on the other hand, were harder to decipher, obscured by the fog of his withdrawal. Yet even in his silence, he could sense a yearning. He'd seen how his son's eyes lit up when he spoke of the space exploration documentaries they sometimes watched together, and the quiet awe that flickered across his face as he described the vastness of the universe. He'd also noticed the detailed drawings of fantastical creatures and intricate machinery that began to fill Kofi's sketchbooks, worlds of his own creation where logic and order prevailed, a stark contrast to the chaos of his daily life. It was as if Kofi believed that by mastering the complexities of these imagined realms, he could somehow gain control and create a sanctuary for himself, a place where the unpredictable storms of his parents' conflict could not penetrate.

He dreamt not of conquering dragons or exploring distant galaxies, but of finding a place of peace, a quiet corner of the world where he could exist without the constant threat of emotional fallout.

He recalled a conversation with Maya just a few weeks earlier. They had been discussing her upcoming exams, a subject that usually sparked a mix of anxiety and determination in her. This time, however, her response had been tinged with an unusual weariness. "It's just… if I do well, Papa," she'd said, her gaze fixed on a point beyond his shoulder, "if I get into a good university, then maybe… then maybe things will be better. Maybe you and Mama will have more time, you know, to not argue."

The unspoken implication hung heavy in the air: her academic success was the key, the magic wand that would restore happiness to their fractured home. He had wanted to tell her that grades did not measure her worth, that her peace was not contingent on their reconciliation, but the words had caught in his throat, choked by the overwhelming weight of his own culpability. He was the architect of this environment, the one who had promised them a safe harbour, only to let the waves of discord batter its walls.

Kofi’s responses to his father's attempts at conversation were always polite, brief, and unrevealing, forming a barrier that protected his inner world. Despite Kofi's detached politeness and unresponsive demeanour, his occasional moments of withdrawal, like at dinner when he shrugged and mumbled, revealed a child resigned to silence and concealment of pain.

The guilt was a constant, gnawing ache. He saw the subtle yet significant ways the relentless friction between him and their mother was shaping their childhoods. Maya, the bright spark, was being forged into a diamond under immense pressure, her brilliance tempered by an almost unbearable need to prove herself and earn a happiness that should have been an inherent right. Kofi, the sensitive soul, was retreating into himself, his spirit dulled by constant exposure to conflict, his dreams taking flight into worlds far removed from the reality of his home.

He had brought them to a new country, promising them opportunity and a better future. He had envisioned a life of prosperity, growth, and shared joys. Instead, he had inadvertently created an environment that eroded their innocence, amplifying their childhood anxieties and reshaping their dreams under the desperate need for parental peace. He saw the reflection of his failures in their altered behaviour, in Maya's careful calculations of ambition, and in Kofi's profound stillness. He was a father who had promised them the moon and stars, only to find himself presiding over a sky filled with storm clouds, the echoes of his own discord the soundtrack to their lost childhoods. The weight of this realisation was almost unbearable, a heavy cloak he could not shed, a constant reminder of the unintended consequences of his fractured life.

THE SEEDS OF THE FUTURE

Their lives in London were shaping a new identity distinct from that of their homeland through a subtle, unconscious process of assimilation. Maya and Kofi absorbed the rhythms and colours of their environment, gradually becoming 'third culture kids'- living between their Nigerian heritage and British upbringing. This duality was more than external; it was a profound internal shift, transforming their sense of belonging, family, and the world.

Maya was absorbing London like a sponge. Her academic pursuits, while driven by the anxieties of her home life, were also opening new intellectual horizons. The British education system, with its emphasis on critical thinking and diverse perspectives, was challenging her to view the world through multiple lenses.

She devoured books on cultures, histories, and ways of being. Her vocabulary expanded to include British colloquialisms and social nuance. Navigating bustling tube stations with ease, she sought information, connection, and her next destination. Learning to code-switch between formal English and relaxed slang, she gained insight into London's multicultural fabric, understanding family traditions, hybrid identities, and shared experiences. Maya found friendship, proud of her Nigerian roots, sharing proverbs and flavours such as jollof rice. Her thoughts and aspirations became more London-focused, shifting from pleasing her parents to succeeding and carving her place in the city.

London's environment was shaping Kofi. Its anonymity and size sheltered him and allowed him to disappear into crowds. London also provided new avenues of expression that his past lacked.

He discovered vibrant street art that spoke a language of rebellion and creativity, found solace in the hushed reverence of the British Museum, where ancient stories whispered from millennia past, and was captivated by the digital landscapes of online gaming communities that transcended geographical boundaries.

These communities were made up of individuals who shared his passion for strategy, offered him a sense of belonging, and a place where his quiet intensity was not only accepted but celebrated. He learned to articulate his ideas in writing, and his forum posts became eloquent expressions of his strategic mind and imaginative flair. While he remained reserved in face-to-face interactions, his online persona blossomed, a testament to his inner richness. He was absorbing the subtle nuances of British politeness, the art of understated humour, and the layering of conversations with unspoken meanings.

He was learning to observe, listen, and interpret the world with a discerning eye, skills sharpened by his need to navigate the complexities of his home environment. His Nigerian heritage, while less overt than Maya's, remained present. He cherished the few remaining Nigerian books in his father's study, the worn covers holding stories that felt like whispers from a distant past. He sometimes hummed traditional Nigerian melodies, a quiet, almost unconscious expression of his lineage. But his dreams were increasingly taking on a distinctly British tone, partly influenced by the narratives he encountered in films, books, and the very air of this new city.

The foundations of their future selves were laid in these formative years in London. Challenges such as unspoken tensions at home, academic pressures, and the task of navigating two cultures weren't just obstacles but the very materials forging their resilience and perspectives. Maya's drive, shaped by these experiences, would likely become formidable. Her ability to connect with diverse people, developed through her interactions and immersion in London's multicultural environment, would serve her well globally. She was learning to be a bridge-builder and a cultural translator, navigating human interaction with intelligence and empathy. Her understanding expanded beyond her immediate experience to a broader vision.

Kofi's quiet introspection, coupled with his burgeoning technical skills and imaginative capacity, held immense potential. The patience and observation he cultivated for self-preservation were now channelled into a deep understanding of systems, logic, and the intricate workings of the digital world. His ability to create and inhabit his own constructed realities within games and online communities suggested a capacity for innovation and problem-solving that was deeply valuable.

He was learning to communicate effectively, even if primarily in written form, a skill that was increasingly crucial in the modern world. His sensitivity, once perceived as a vulnerability, was becoming a source of empathy and a unique perspective that could enrich his interactions and his creative endeavours. He was a quiet observer deeply attuned to the underlying currents of the world around him, a trait that often led to profound insights.

Their dual cultural immersion wasn't about choosing one identity but about creating a synthesis—a richer, more complex self. They appreciated the storytelling, community, and vibrant expressions of their Nigerian heritage while embracing the opportunities and forward-looking ethos of their British upbringing. London, diverse and ever-changing, was the perfect place for this transformation, offering space to explore and define themselves. They planted the seeds of future identities amid the busy streets, quiet libraries, and digital landscapes. They grew into young adults carrying echoes of two worlds, a testament to their resilience, adaptability, and family strength amid challenges.

Although their journeys diverged in their immediate manifestations, they were leading them towards a deeper understanding of who they were and who they were destined to become, shaped by the unique confluence of their Nigerian roots and their London lives. The city, in its own way, was becoming an integral part of their personal narratives, a silent witness to their growth and their evolving sense of self.

CHAPTER 7
THE WIFE'S PERSPECTIVE UNVEILED

BENEATH THE SURFACE OF STRENGTH

The quiet hum of the washing machine was a familiar, almost unnoticed sound in the small flat, a stark contrast to the buzz of anxieties that often filled Amina's mind. She watched the clothes tumble, as if mirroring the chaotic rotation of her thoughts. It was a scene of family life, a picture of a wife managing her household, but beneath the surface, a storm was gathering. The London dream, the glittering promise that had beckoned them across continents, had begun to fray at the edges, revealing a harsher, more demanding reality. It was not the life she had envisioned, not the serene haven where her husband's ambition would blossom unhindered and her own sacrifices would be met with effortless gratitude. Instead, it was a constant, worrying pressure, a relentless calculus of pounds and pence, of needs versus wants, of dreams deferred and realities faced with a weary sigh.

She remembered the excitement, the sense of hope that had filled their home in Lagos as they prepared for this grand adventure. London, with its storied history, its opportunities, and its promise of a better future for their children, had felt like a gateway to a new existence. Now, the gateway had led them to a cramped flat, the air thick with the scent of damp and compromise, the sky perpetually grey. The sheer cost of everything was a daily shock. A loaf of bread, a carton of milk, a child's shoes. Each purchase felt like a slight erosion of their carefully constructed stability.

Her husband, blessed with an optimism that thrived on oblivion, saw the sacrifices as temporary, necessary stepping stones. He spoke of future successes, of promotions, of a time when this struggle would be a distant memory. But Amina felt the weight of the present, the immediate, pressing needs that demanded her attention, her resourcefulness, her relentless vigilance.

Her sharp words and the impatience that sometimes flared were not born of malice but of a profound, bone-deep weariness. It was the weary cry of a captain steering a ship through treacherous waters, where every decision carried consequences, where a single misstep could send them crashing against unseen ridges. She saw the dreams in her children's eyes, the innocent belief in a future still unwritten, and the responsibility to protect that innocence, to ensure that the harsh realities of their new life did not extinguish their youthful exuberance.

The cultural differences, too, were a constant, subtle source of friction. In Nigeria, the community had been a tangible, interwoven force. Neighbours offered help without being asked, and extended families provided a safety net to share life's burdens. Here, in the anonymity of London, a profound sense of isolation had settled upon her. The polite nods from neighbours, the brief exchanges with shopkeepers – these were passing interactions, devoid of the warmth and connection she craved. She missed the easy camaraderie of women sharing gossip over chores, the comforting rhythm of communal prayer, and the spontaneous invitations to share a meal. Here, she was an outsider, a visitor in a land whose customs and social codes remained elusive. It was a puzzle she struggled to decipher.

Her English, once a source of pride, now felt inadequate, clumsy, and insufficient to express the depth of her feelings and the reasons for her concerns. She would rehearse conversations in her head, searching for the right words and the most diplomatic phrasing, only to have them stumble out in a rush of frustration when the moment arrived. The fear of miscommunication that could accidentally offend was a constant companion, adding another layer of anxiety to her already overloaded mental landscape. She longed for the familiarity of her own language and the effortless flow of conversation that had once been as natural as breathing.

Her husband's work, while providing the income that kept them afloat, also demanded a significant portion of his energy, attention, and presence. He would return home late, his mind scanning his day's performance for any errors. While she understood the necessity of his efforts, the long hours left her often alone to navigate the complexities of their new life. The school runs, the homework help, the comforting of restless children – these were her domain, tasks she undertook with diligence, but with a growing sense of loneliness. She yearned for shared moments of reflection, for a partner to brainstorm solutions with, for a hand to hold as they faced the unknown together.

The perceived harshness in her interactions with the children, the sharp reprimands that sometimes punctuated their days, were outward manifestations of this internal struggle. It was the frustration of a mother trying to instil values, maintain discipline, and guide her children through a world that felt increasingly alien, while battling her own insecurities and fears. She saw their vulnerability, their openness to the influences of their new environment, and a fierce protective instinct, honed by years of nurturing, flare within her. Sometimes, that instinct manifested as sternness, a desire to shield them from the very uncertainties that plagued her. She wanted them to be strong, resilient, to possess the quiet fortitude she herself was striving to cultivate. But in her haste, in her overwhelming sense of responsibility, she sometimes forgot to offer them the solace, the unconditional warmth that a child truly needs.

She watched Maya, with her increasing independence and quick mind, and felt a sense of pride mixed with a surge of apprehension. Maya was adapting, thriving even, in ways that Amina found both admirable and slightly scary. Her daughter's embrace of this new culture, her growing fluency in the language, her friendships with girls from diverse backgrounds – it was all a testament to her adaptability. But Amina also worried. Was Maya losing a piece of herself in this process? Was she forgetting the values and traditions ingrained in their heritage? The subtle shifts in Maya's language, the adoption of new slang, and the way she spoke of her friends' homes with a casual ease all contributed to a growing sense of distance. Amina longed to connect with her daughter on a deeper level, to understand the world through her eyes, but the widening gap in experience often made such intimacy feel just out of reach.

Kofi, in his quiet way, faced a different kind of challenge. His withdrawn nature and tendency to retreat into his own world had always been a source of concern. Now, in the isolating embrace of London, those traits felt amplified. She saw him glued to his computer screen, his eyes alight with a passion that seemed to extend beyond the confines of their small flat. She knew he was engaging with others and building connections online, but she couldn't shake the feeling that he was drifting further away from her and the family. She tried to draw him out, to engage him in conversations about his day and his interests, but his responses were often brief, his gaze still fixed on the glowing screen. Her frustration would bubble, and she would sometimes snap at him, her voice sharper than intended, only to meet a bewildered silence that deepened her sense of helplessness. She wanted to be the mother who understood, the mother who could guide her son through the complexities of adolescence, but she felt perpetually on the outside, gazing in.

The dream of London had not been a lie, not entirely. It was still a city of immense possibility, vibrant culture, and opportunity. But the reality of making that dream real was proving to be a far more arduous and often solitary undertaking than she had ever imagined. The weight of managing the household, navigating the cultural landscape, and nurturing her children fell disproportionately on her shoulders. Her husband, caught in the relentless current of his own ambitions, was often too preoccupied to fully grasp the extent of her daily battles. And so Amina soldiered on, her strength a carefully constructed facade, her anxieties a silent, persistent ache, all in the hope that one day the shimmering promise of London would finally materialise into a life that felt less like a struggle and more like a home. She was the anchor, holding their family steady in the spinning currents of their new existence. Her resilience was a silent testament to a love that ran deeper than any fear, any hardship.

The promises whispered in Lagos's sunset had been potent. Woven from threads of ambition and a fervent belief in a brighter tomorrow, spun by her husband's confident voice. He had painted a London not just of opportunities but of abundance, a place where their children would soar, unburdened by the limitations they themselves had known. Amina had absorbed these narratives, not just as a wife listening to her husband, but as a woman who understood the unspoken societal contract of migration. It was a testament to a man's capability, a family's resilience, and a nation's yearning for recognition on the global stage. The image he'd conjured was one of effortless ascent, a steady climb towards a plateau of comfort and achievement, where their names were engraved. She, too, had contributed to this tapestry of aspiration, believing in the shared vision and the collective push towards a better life. She had seen herself as the quiet force behind his triumphs, the steadfast foundation upon which his grandeur would be built. The sacrifices, she had understood implicitly, were not just hers but a shared investment in this grand, unfolding narrative.

But the reality of London was a stark, brutal counterpoint to those romanticised visions. It was a city that demanded a pound of flesh for every crumb of comfort. The hushed conversations about dwindling savings, the meticulous tracking of every penny spent on essentials – these were the discordant notes that shattered the melodious dream. Amina found herself in a constant, internal negotiation, a silent battle against the rising tide of anxiety. Every grocery bill, every utility statement, felt like a small, personal defeat. She remembered her husband's words, spoken with such conviction: "Amina, this is temporary. A few years of sacrifice, and we will reap the rewards. Our children will have the best education, the best opportunities." He spoke of future dividends, of a time when their current struggles would be merely anecdotes, colourful tales to impress future generations. He saw the present as a dark tunnel, but he fixed his gaze on the distant light at its end.

Amina, however, was trapped in the tunnel's depths. The light seemed impossibly distant, and the darkness pressed in, heavy and suffocating. Her role, once defined by a shared vision of prosperity, had morphed into something far more immediate and desperate: survival. The abstract concept of "opportunity" had been replaced by the concrete need to keep the lights on, ensure there was enough food on the table, and prevent the fear of destitution from taking root. This shift in focus was not a conscious decision but an emergent property of their circumstances. The grand narrative of migration had been reduced to a series of urgent, granular tasks, each demanding her full and unyielding attention.

The societal narratives she had absorbed back home, the stories of immigrants who had "made it," who had overcome impossible odds through sheer determination, now served as both inspiration and relentless pressure. She saw her husband as the embodiment of that driven immigrant, pushing forward, his eyes on the prize. But she also saw the immense personal cost, not just to him but to their family and, increasingly, to herself. The weight of his ambition, once a source of shared pride, now felt like an oppressive burden, placed squarely on her shoulders. She was acutely aware that the success he chased was linked to their collective well-being. If he failed, if his ventures faltered, the repercussions would be catastrophic. This awareness fuelled a fierce, almost desperate pragmatism within her.

This pragmatism, however, began to manifest in ways that felt increasingly constricting for her and her family. Her focus narrowed, sharpening on the immediate and the tangible. The dreams for her children, once expansive and colourful, began to shrink, redefined by what was achievable within their current financial constraints. The desire for them to attend the most prestigious schools and to take part in every extracurricular activity was tempered by the reality of tuition fees and the cost of dance lessons or football kits. She found herself scrutinising every request, every wish, through a lens of pure economic feasibility. "Is this a necessity, or a luxury?" became her silent mantra.

Her husband, in the relentless pursuit of his professional goals, often seemed to float above these daily calculations. He would come home, tired but buoyed by small professional victories, and speak of future investments and long-term strategies. He would talk about a time when they could afford a larger home, when the children could pursue any interest without financial impediment. Amina would listen, her hands busy with dinner preparations. His optimism, once a comforting balm, now felt like a painful disconnect. His "future" was a distant country, while her "present" was a land of rationing and calculated compromises.

She found herself becoming the gatekeeper of their finances, the stern administrator of their limited resources. It wasn't that she didn't trust her husband; instead, she felt she was the only one truly grounded in their precarious financial reality. His eyes fixed on the horizon; hers scanned the immediate terrain for pitfalls. This meant she often had to be the one to say "no." A new toy for Kofi, an outing with Maya and her friends, a small indulgence for herself – all were subjected to her rigorous internal audit. The thrill of a spontaneous purchase, the simple joy of gifting without calculation, became a distant memory.

She began to hoard, not in the traditional sense, but in a psychological one. Every penny saved felt like a victory against the encroaching tide of uncertainty. She'd buy non-perishable goods in bulk when they were on offer, stretching their budget. She'd mend clothes that were still wearable rather than replacing them. She'd meticulously plan meals to minimise waste. These actions, born of necessity, began to shape her identity. She was no longer just a wife and mother; she was the Chief Financial Officer of their struggling household, the vigilant guardian of their dwindling reserves.

This intense focus on financial prudence, while ensuring their immediate survival, also began to cast a shadow over their lives. Her husband, accustomed to a certain level of spending freedom back home, sometimes felt irritated by her unyielding control. "Amina," he'd say, his voice tinged with exasperation, "it's just a small thing. Don't we deserve a little enjoyment?" And she would reply, her voice steady, though her heart ached with the effort, "We have to be careful, Kayode. We don't know what tomorrow will bring." The unspoken fear was always there, a silent spectre at their dinner table: the fear that their sacrifices would be in vain, that they would have uprooted themselves, endured all the hardship, only to end up no better off, or even worse, than before.

The societal expectations for her children weighed heavily on her. She wanted them to be academically successful and to secure bright futures, not just for their sake but as validation for all the sacrifices they were making. If they excelled and went on to achieve great things, every difficult day, every strained conversation about money, would feel justified. This desire for their success became almost an obsession, driving her to be overly strict. She saw their schooling as their primary contribution to the family's future, their passport to a better life. Therefore, any perceived distraction or deviation from their academic path was viewed with suspicion and met with firm disapproval.

She remembered a time when Kofi had been fascinated by a new hobby, a budding interest in drawing. He would spend hours sketching, his forehead wrinkled in concentration, a quiet joy radiating from him. Amina, however, had seen it as a drain on his precious study time. "Kofi," she'd said, her voice sharp, "you need to focus on your maths. Drawing will not get you into a good university." The light in his eyes had dimmed, replaced by a familiar, resigned look. She regretted it almost immediately, as the harshness of her tone snuffed out his innocent passion. But the fear, the overriding need for security and success, had won out. Her pragmatism, her dedication to ensuring their sacrifices were not in vain, was slowly and inevitably shaping her into a figure of authority rather than one of nurturing comfort.

Maya, too, felt the pinch of her mother's heightened vigilance. While Amina admired Maya's growing independence and her ability to navigate the complexities of adolescence in a new country, she also constantly worried about Maya's choices. Every outing with friends, every late-night conversation with a new acquaintance, was a source of apprehension. Was Maya making the right friends? Was she being exposed to influences that could derail her future? The fear that her daughter might stray from the path or succumb to temptations that could jeopardise their hard-won stability led Amina to impose strict rules and constant questioning.

Maya's desire for a social life and everyday teenage experiences often clashed with Amina's overriding need for control and security. The whispered conversations between mother and daughter were laced with tension, unfulfilled wishes, and unspoken anxieties.

Amina's own aspirations, once vibrant and personal, had been subsumed by the family's needs. She'd dreamed of further education, perhaps returning to her passion for literature, but the demands of their new life had pushed those desires to the furthest reaches of her consciousness. There was simply no time, no mental space, for such self-indulgence. Her energy was consumed by the immediate needs of survival and the relentless pursuit of a stable future for her children. Her world had shrunk to the confines of their flat, the school gates, and the marketplace. The broader aspects of life – art, culture, personal growth – felt like luxuries she could no longer afford.

She felt a growing distance from her husband. He was the visionary, the one who spoke of the grand design, while she was the pragmatist, meticulously managing the building blocks. His optimism, though often ungrounded in the immediate realities, was essential to his drive. But her realism, though vital for their survival, sometimes felt like a dampener on his spirit and their children's. She recognised this but felt powerless to change.

The weight of unmet expectations – not just her husband's, but her own, and crucially, the unspoken expectations of a society that judged immigrant success so harshly – was a constant presence. She was no longer simply a wife; she was the fortification against ruin, the fiercely protective mother, and the reluctant accountant of their precarious existence, all rolled into one, a solitary figure battling the tides of uncertainty, unyielding resolve, driven by the desperate need to prove that their colossal leap of faith had not been in vain.

CULTURAL SCRIPTS AND GENDER ROLES

The culture back home, in the vibrant heart of Nigeria, had offered a comforting, albeit sometimes rigid, framework for Amina's understanding of family and gender roles. She had grown up on a steady diet of narratives that underscored the man's position as the undisputed provider, the architect of the family's material well-being. His was the public sphere, the arena of earning and ambition, while hers was the private domain – the sanctuary of home, the nurturing of children, and the smooth running of domestic affairs. It was not a notion of subservience, but rather one of complementary strengths, a divinely ordained division of labour that ensured the family unit functioned with a cordial rhythm. The wife's duty was to create a haven, be the bedrock of support, and manage the intricate details of household logistics so that the husband could focus, unburdened, on his crucial role as the family's financial anchor. She had internalised these scripts deeply, seeing her own role as essential, noble, and intrinsically tied to the success and stability of her husband and children. Her efforts in managing the home, ensuring the children were well-fed and educated, and making her husband feel supported and cherished, were not mere chores but sacred duties.

The stark economic realities of their new life demanded a recalibration, a reinterpretation of these familiar roles. The expectation that Kayode would be the sole financial engine while she managed the domestic side was proving increasingly unsustainable. The sheer cost of living in the UK, exorbitant rents, and the high price of everyday necessities meant that Kayode's singular income, even with his diligent efforts, was often stretched to its breaking point.

This reality began to trigger a subtle but significant shift in Amina's perception of her own worth and her right to participate in financial decision-making. If the family's survival hinged on every single penny, and if she was the one meticulously tracking, managing, and stretching those pennies, did that not grant her a voice, perhaps even a louder voice, in how those pennies were allocated? The traditional script suggested she should manage within the budget provided. Yet the sheer effort and sacrifice involved in creating that budget and finding ways to make ends meet fostered a growing sense of agency. She was not merely a passive recipient of funds; she was an active architect of their financial survival, and with that realisation came an unspoken demand for greater involvement.

Amina observed the dynamics of other immigrant families around her. While she didn't actively seek to mimic them, she couldn't help but notice patterns that seemed to contribute to their perceived success. Some families, particularly those in which both partners worked, navigated financial pressures more easily.

She saw women contributing significantly to household income, not as a sign of their husbands' inability to provide, but as a pragmatic strategy for collective advancement. These women, she noted, often took a more assertive stance in family discussions about finances and plans. They seemed to possess a confidence that stemmed from their tangible contribution and their dual roles as homemakers and breadwinners. Was this the future of immigrant families in this new land? Was the traditional Nigerian model, so cherished and familiar, becoming archaic in the face of London's relentless demands? The thought lingered, a seed of doubt planted in the fertile ground of her anxieties. She began to wonder whether her own adherence to the older script, while rooted in cultural pride, was inadvertently holding her family back, preventing them from fully leveraging their collective potential in this new environment.

Subtle yet persistent societal expectations in the UK complicated this internal debate. While the UK championed ideals of gender equality, the lived reality for many women, particularly immigrant women, often presented a confused picture. Amina sometimes felt caught between two worlds, with her Nigerian upbringing clashing with her perceptions of British society. She saw women in the UK working in diverse roles, with seemingly greater autonomy and influence. Yet she also observed societal pressures that, in many ways, still placed the primary burden of childcare and domestic responsibilities on women, regardless of their employment status. This created a complex interplay of expectations: a desire to emulate the perceived independence of British women, while still feeling the pull of her deeply ingrained Nigerian responsibilities. The notion of her financial contribution in the UK wasn't just about her own society; it was also about aligning herself with what she perceived as a more modern, perhaps more successful, way of life in this new country.

The weight of Kayode's ambition, once a shared dream, now also contributed to this re-evaluation. He was driven and relentless in his pursuit of a better life, and Amina admired that fiercely. But his singular focus meant that the day-to-day management of their financial precariousness often fell to her. When he spoke of investments, his language was optimistic, forward-looking, and usually detached from the immediate, granular concerns of making ends meet. Amina, by contrast, was immersed in the reality of utility bills, grocery prices, and school trip fees. Her constant vigilance over their spending, her careful budgeting and meticulous saving, were not acts of control born of suspicion, but of necessity. She was the gatekeeper of their immediate survival, and this role, she felt, entitled her to a greater say in the family's financial direction. The traditional script of the man as the sole financial commander, while still respected in principle, felt increasingly out of sync with the practical demands of their situation.

This growing sense of her own entitlement to a more significant role in financial governance was not a rebellion against Kayode, but rather an evolution shaped by circumstance. She was not seeking to usurp his authority, but to share the burden and the decision-making. She understood that in Nigeria, a wife's involvement in financial decision-making is unusual, or even a sign of her husband's weakness.

However, the UK was a different landscape, and the survival of her family in this new terrain demanded a more collaborative, perhaps even a more egalitarian, approach to financial management. Her meticulous tracking of every penny and her innovative ways of stretching their budget were not just about saving money; they were about demonstrating her competence, strategic thinking, and indispensable contribution to their collective well-being. She felt that her efforts deserved recognition, not just a pat on the back, but a more equitable share in the family's financial strategy.

The children, too, became a catalyst for this shift. Amina's fierce desire for them to succeed and have the best education and opportunities meant she was intimately involved in every aspect of their schooling and development. She understood that their academic achievements were crucial not only for their future but also as a validation of the immense sacrifices the entire family was making. This deep involvement in their educational journey naturally extended to the financial implications of that journey, the cost of tutors, the expense of extracurricular activities, and the necessity of providing a stable home environment conducive to study.

This practical engagement with the financial requirements of their children's future solidified her understanding of their financial situation and her own capacity to contribute to its management. She wasn't just a passive observer of Kayode's financial plans; she was an active participant in the very engine of their family's upward mobility, and that role demanded a more prominent voice.

She often found herself subtly guiding Kayode's financial discussions, not by dictating but by presenting her meticulously gathered data. She would show him spreadsheets detailing their monthly expenses, highlighting areas for savings, and outlining the projected costs of future educational needs.

These presentations were not confrontational; they were collaborative efforts, her contribution to their shared vision. She was demonstrating her financial acumen, her understanding of their present reality, and her foresight for their future. It was her way of asserting her rightful place in the economic discourse, a place earned through tireless effort and unwavering dedication. The cultural script that relegated her to the domestic sphere was being rewritten by the pragmatism of their new environment, by the undeniable evidence of her capabilities, and by the shared imperative to secure a prosperous future for their children.

The challenge, however, lay in articulating this evolving role without causing undue friction. Traditional Nigerian gender roles, while perhaps less pronounced in the UK, still held a particular cultural resonance, a trace that could be easily disturbed. Amina was acutely aware of this. She didn't want Kayode to feel emasculated or undermined. She aimed to foster a partnership and shared responsibility rather than a challenge to his authority. This meant carefully choosing her words and framing her contributions not as criticisms but as supportive insights. She would often preface her financial observations with phrases like, "Kayode, I've been thinking about our budget for Kofi's secondary school fees," or "Darling, I've noticed we could save money on our grocery bills if we planned our meals more carefully." This approach allowed her to inject her practical wisdom into their financial planning without directly confronting the traditional expectations of his role as the primary provider.

She also recognised that her internal script was in flux. The confidence she gained from successfully managing their household on a tight budget and from her ability to find creative solutions to financial challenges was gradually chipping away at the ingrained sense of deference that had characterised her interactions about finances back home.

This newfound self-assurance was not arrogance but a quiet pride in her resilience and resourcefulness. She saw herself not just as a wife and mother but as a capable manager, a strategic thinker, and a crucial pillar of their new life in Britain. This internal shift was perhaps the most significant, as it empowered her to advocate for her rightful place in the family's financial narrative. This narrative was no longer solely Kayode's to write. The cultural scripts were still there, a faint echo of the past. Still, the reality of their present and the hopeful horizon of their future demanded a new language, a new set of rules, and a new understanding of her indispensable role.

LONELINESS AND THE LOSS OF SUPPORT SYSTEMS

The silence of their London flat, particularly in the quiet hours when Kayode's work kept him away, often pressed in on Amina with a weight she hadn't anticipated. Back in Lagos, even during moments of solitary reflection, familiar sounds were always there – the distant chatter of neighbours, the rumble of traffic, the calls of street vendors. And more importantly, there was the ever-present hum of connection. Her mother, her sisters, a network of aunts and cousins, friends who were as close as family – they formed a vibrant, ever-present chorus that underscored every aspect of her life.

A casual visit, a shared pot of soup, a whispered worry passed over a fence, a spontaneous gathering for tea – these were the threads that wove the fabric of her social existence, providing a cushion against the sharp edges of life. When sadness or uncertainty visited, there was always a hand to hold, a shoulder to lean on, a shared laugh that could chase away the shadows. Support was not something one actively sought; it was an ambient presence, as natural and essential as the air she breathed.

Here, in this collapsing, indifferent metropolis, that rhythm had been replaced by a disconcerting quietness. The phone calls, though frequent at first, began to feel like echoes from a distant land, a tantalising reminder of what was absent rather than a substitute for it. The intimacy of shared space, the ability to knock on a neighbour's door for a cup of sugar and end up sharing an hour of conversation, was gone. The sheer scale of London, with its millions of inhabitants, paradoxically amplified her sense of isolation. Each person seemed to be on their own trajectory, caught up in their own pursuits and orbits. The easy company she had known, the ingrained habit of community, felt like a forgotten language.

Kayode, bless his heart, was her anchor in this foreign sea, but his very dedication to their new life deepened her solitude. His days were a relentless march from dawn till late into the night, his mind often consumed by the pressures of his new role, the intricate dance of his career, and the weight of his responsibility for their family's future. He would return home, weary, his shoulders curved with the day's burdens. While his love for her was evident in his gentle touch and reassuring words, he was often too exhausted to be the companion her soul craved. Their conversations, when they happened, were often functional – reports on the children's day, discussions about bills, brief recaps of their respective struggles.

The deep, soul-baring exchanges, the sharing of vulnerabilities, the quiet comfort of simply being together without the need for words, had become a luxury they could rarely afford. He was her survival partner, but the shared emotional landscape, the space where they could truly nurture each other's spirits, felt increasingly distant.

This profound sense of loneliness, this void where companionship and emotional solace should have been, began to manifest in subtle ways. Amina, who had always found joy in nurturing others and maintaining harmony in her home, now found herself grappling with an internal emptiness. Without the constant external validation of a supportive community, her sense of self began to feel less grounded. The absence of familiar faces and the lack of shared experiences focused solely on immediate survival needs left her feeling worried. She would watch the children, her beautiful

Kofi and little Maya, their laughter a balm to her spirit, but even their presence couldn't fill the gap. They were her reason for being, her driving force, but they were also her responsibility, and in their innocent dependence she saw a reflection of her own vulnerability.

It was in this fertile ground of isolation that her focus on the tangible – on finances and the meticulous management of their household – intensified. When emotional sustenance was scarce, the need to control the physical and material aspects of her life became paramount. Her days, once filled with a social rhythm, now stretched before her, vast and unstructured, save for the duties of childcare and the running of their home. The budget, the grocery lists, the meticulous tracking of every penny, and the constant vigilance over utility bills – these became her battlegrounds, the arenas where she could exert her will and find a sense of accomplishment.

In a world that felt increasingly unstable and unpredictable, where her emotional needs went unmet, the quantifiable became a source of security. It heightened her focus on practical matters. When loneliness threatened to overwhelm, when the yearning for a familiar voice or a comforting embrace became too acute, Amina could immerse herself in the mundane, the immediate, the solvable. The intricate puzzle of making their income last until the end of the month, planning healthy and affordable meals, and organising the children's school activities.

These tasks demanded her full attention, pushing back the encroaching shadows of her emotional state. It was a coping mechanism, a way of self-preservation, born of a deep-seated need to feel secure and in control when so much else felt beyond her grasp. The tangible, the concrete, offered readily available solace, unlike the elusive comfort of human connection, so desperately needed.

Her husband's long working hours, while understandable and a testament to his commitment, inadvertently created a vacuum that she felt compelled to fill with her own efforts. He was their provider, the engine of their material progress, and she respected that immensely. But in his absence, and without her own established network, the emotional labour of their family fell squarely on her shoulders.

She was the constant, the unwavering presence for the children, the one who ensured the wheels of their domestic life kept turning smoothly. Yet this constant giving, this steadfast dedication to the practicalities of their existence, left little room for her own replenishment. The emotional reserves, like their financial ones, were constantly drawn upon, with little opportunity for replenishment.

She often stood by the window, watching families pass by in the park, their easy laughter and shared glances a stark contrast to her own internal landscape. It was a pang of envy, sharp and unexpected, followed by a wave of self-reproach. Why should she feel this way? She had her children and a husband who worked tirelessly for them. Yet the deep, inherent human need for connection, for shared vulnerability, for the simple comfort of belonging, could not be so easily dismissed. Loneliness, she was discovering, was a relentless thief, capable of stealing joy, energy, and even a sense of self-worth. In the vastness of London, in the quiet of their flat, Amina was learning its insidious power firsthand. This profound sense of isolation, coupled with the weight of her responsibilities, meant that her reliance on the tangible, on the measurable achievements of household management and financial prudence, became not just a strategy for security but a vital lifeline in the turbulent waters of her new life.

It was in these meticulously managed details that she found a semblance of order, a quiet triumph, and a way to navigate the overwhelming emotional terrain of her uprooted existence.

THE REVALUATION OF SUCCESS

Was success measured solely by pounds and pence, by the net worth of their bank accounts? Or did it encompass the less quantifiable, more transient elements that truly made a life rich? Amina thought of her mother's home in Lagos. This place rarely boasted an overflowing savings account but was perpetually rich in warmth, laughter, and the easy company of neighbours who felt like family. It was a place to resolve issues over a meal and to air worries over cups of tea, where a helping hand was as natural as breathing. There, success had been defined by community, connection, and the deep, abiding sense of belonging. Here, in London, they had financial security, but were they truly thriving? Were they happy?

The question worried her. She had uprooted herself, her children, and her entire world, chasing a dream that now seemed to be morphing into something entirely different. The dream wasn't just about material comfort; it was about building a good life, a fulfilling life, a life where her family could flourish not only financially but also emotionally. And if the relentless pursuit of financial security was inadvertently eroding their emotional well-being, what was the true cost of this "success"?

Her attempts to economise and her obsessive focus on frugality were not born of greed but of a deep-seated fear. A fear that if she didn't control the tangible, the measurable, everything else would unravel. With Kayode consumed by work, the children grappling with the complexities of a new school and culture, and her own support system thousands of miles away, the budget became her battlefield. Each saving was a small act of defiance against the chaos, a tiny island of control in a sea of uncertainty. It was a way of saying, "I am still in charge. I am still capable."

She remembered the sheer panic that had gripped her in the first few months, when she'd realised how much more expensive everything was. The cost of basic groceries, rent, and utilities – it was a shock to the system. Kayode, bless him, had reassured her, reminding her of his salary and their calculated financial plan. But ingrained habits of scarcity, the memory of making do and making things last, were hard to shake. So she doubled down. She became an expert coupon clipper, a connoisseur of supermarket sales, and a magician at transforming leftovers into new culinary creations. She learned to mend clothes rather than replace them, to repair rather than discard.

These were not just acts of saving; they were acts of self-preservation. In a life where so much felt beyond her control, mastering the art of making their money work harder gave her a sense of relevance. It was a concrete achievement, a measurable success she could hold in her hands. When she managed to stretch their weekly food budget by an extra ten pounds, it felt like a triumph. It was a small victory against the overwhelming forces of their new environment, a validation of her efforts and resourcefulness. She wasn't just a wife and mother but also a financial strategist and a domestic engineer.

But the hollowness persisted. Amina yearned to offer them more than just a financially secure home. She longed to pour her emotional energy into them, to be the steady, unburdened presence they deserved. But often, by the time Kayode returned, the day's meticulous management had drained her emotional well: their finances, the endless calculations, the constant vigilance.

Her re-evaluation of success was not sudden but a slow, simmering realisation, a dawning awareness that the definition she had brought with her was incomplete. It prioritised the external, the visible, over the internal. She had achieved financial stability, yes. But at what cost to her family's harmony, to her own sense of self, to the very joy of living? The children were well-fed, well-clothed, and safe. They had access to a good education. These were undeniable blessings. Yet there was a subtle but pervasive sense of disconnection she couldn't shake.

The laughter she heard from other families in the park and the easy banter she sometimes overheard painted a picture of a different kind of success – one intertwined with shared experiences, spontaneous moments of joy, and a deep sense of belonging. She saw mothers who seemed to have more time, not necessarily less financial pressure, but a different allocation of their energy. They appeared fully present for their children, engaging in conversations that weren't solely about homework or upcoming tests, but about their feelings, their dreams, and their everyday observations.

Amina's days were a careful orchestration of tasks, each meticulously planned to maximise efficiency. Wake the children, prepare breakfast, pack lunches, school run, grocery shopping (always with a list and a price comparison app), household chores, laundry, meal planning, budget review, school pick-up, homework supervision, dinner preparation, bedtime routine. And then, if Kayode wasn't too late, a brief period of hushed conversation before sleep. There was little room for spontaneous outings or leisurely afternoons in the park. Every moment had to be accounted for, optimised, and turned into a productive step towards their defined goal.

She began to feel a deep-seated unease, a quiet rebellion brewing within her. Was she sacrificing the very essence of what it meant to be a family – the richness of shared moments, the unhurried unfolding of everyday life – on the altar of financial security? She hadn't anticipated this. She had believed that with economic stability, the emotional landscape would naturally flourish. But it seemed that emotional well-being, like a delicate plant, required its own form of nurturing, its own specific conditions for growth. And those conditions – time, attention, presence, connection – were precisely what were sacrificed in the relentless pursuit of the tangible.

Her children, though they never complained, sometimes seemed to possess a quiet maturity beyond their years, a self-reliance born of having to navigate many of their challenges independently. She saw it in Maya's persistence when tackling a maths problem and in Kofi's polite but reserved interactions with his peers. She worried that in her quest to provide them with a secure future, she was inadvertently depriving them of a rich present.

She began to question the very definition of the "good life" they had imported. Was it a life of material abundance at the expense of emotional richness? Was it one in which parents were mere providers and facilitators rather than active participants in their children's emotional and social development? The sacrifices Kayode made, the long hours he endured, were for them, for their future. She knew this, but she also understood that a child's future is built not only on a solid financial foundation but also on one of love, connection, and a sense of being seen and heard.

This re-evaluation wasn't about rejecting their progress; it was about recalibrating their compass. It was about understanding that true success in migration wasn't just about arriving at a destination of financial prosperity, but about ensuring that the journey itself nourished the soul and that the new life they were building was rich in all the ways that truly mattered.

The meticulous management of their finances, while a necessary shield, was also, she was beginning to suspect, a cage. A cage that, while protecting them from some external threats, was also limiting their ability to experience the full spectrum of life, the spontaneous joys, and the unscripted moments of connection that made a life truly worth living. She had to find a way to break free, to redefine success not as the absence of struggle, but as the ability to navigate life's challenges with both resilience and grace, with a whole heart as well as a complete bank account.

CHAPTER 8
THE PROTAGONIST'S RECKONING

CONFRONTING THE ILLUSION

The weight of the unspoken had become a physical presence in their small London flat. It was the third occupant, eating at the edges of every conversation, even the silences. Amina's internal reckoning, which had begun as a murmur, was now a roaring current, threatening to pull her under. She looked at Kayode across the dinner table, at the lines of fatigue around his eyes, at the way he mechanically pushed peas around on his plate, his mind clearly miles away, likely in the sterile, fluorescent-lit world of his office. He was the embodiment of their 'Japa' dream, the architect of their material security, yet he was also a stranger in their midst.

It was not the triumphant arrival she had envisioned. It was a slow erosion, a gradual chipping away at the foundations of their joy. The promise of a better life, of opportunities unbounded, had been a siren song, luring them onto the rocks of a reality far harsher than any brochure or well-meaning relative back home had ever conveyed. The 'Japa' dream, she now realised with chilling certainty, was essentially a carefully curated marketing campaign, designed to gloss over the immense emotional and psychological toll of uprooting an entire existence. It was a narrative of upward mobility, of escaping limitations. Still, it rarely spoke of the invisible chains forged in the process – chains of isolation, cultural alienation, and the relentless pressure to prove one's worth in a land that often seemed indifferent to their struggles.

She remembered the feverish excitement of their departure and the anticipation of a fresh start. London, in her imagination, was a gleaming metropolis, a place where hard work met commensurate reward, where their children would breathe the air of opportunity. She'd packed away not just their clothes but also her expectations, a carefully folded quilt of what their life should be. Now that quilt felt worn, its vibrant colours faded, its comforting warmth replaced by a persistent chill. The sheer effort of navigating this new world and the constant vigilance required to stay afloat had left them depleted.

Kayode, once so vibrant and engaged, now moved through his days like a ghost, his presence a matter of logistics rather than connection. His long hours at work, the sacrifices he made – she understood the intention behind them. He was trying to build a fortress for them against the anxieties that had plagued their lives in Nigeria. But in his tireless pursuit of this fortress, he was inadvertently sacrificing the very people he meant to protect. His presence, when he was home, was often a tired echo, his attention fragmented, his conversations a series of updates on bills paid and deadlines met.

The children, Maya and Kofi, bore the brunt of this disconnect. Amina watched them with a growing ache in her chest. They were adapting, yes, their young minds resilient and quick to absorb new customs and a new language. But a subtle, underlying sadness clung to them, a quiet longing for the uninhibited joy of their former lives. They missed the extended family gatherings, the boisterous uncles and aunties, the cousins who were playmates and confidantes. Here, their interactions were more structured, their friendships more carefully navigated. The spontaneous laughter that had once echoed through their Lagos home was now a rare commodity, replaced by polite conversations and scheduled playdates.

Amina's disillusionment was a slow burn, an ash that had smouldered for months, fanned by countless small humiliations and the absence of genuine connection. The initial thrill of their new surroundings had long since worn off, replaced by weary pragmatism. Every trip to the supermarket was a strategic mission, every utility bill a source of anxiety. She had become an expert in frugality, a master of making do, but the victories were hollow. Stretching a budget felt less like an achievement and more like a desperate attempt to plug leaks in a sinking ship.

The dream, she admitted to herself, had been sold on a lie. Or, at the very least, on a significant omission. The glossy advertisements, the aspirational social media posts, the tales of swift success – they all spoke of the destination, the impressive prize. Yet they conveniently sidestepped the brutal, soul-crushing journey. They didn't depict the isolation of a Friday night spent alone while Kayode worked late. They didn't show the quiet desperation of a mother trying to explain to her child why they couldn't afford a small, simple treat. They didn't illustrate the invisible barrier of cultural differences, the microaggressions, or the subtle chipping away at one's sense of belonging.

It was her reckoning. It was the moment when the rose-tinted glasses, meticulously fitted on their arrival, finally shattered, revealing the stark, unvarnished reality beneath. The 'Japa' dream was not a golden ticket to effortless happiness. It was a complex, often painful transformation, a shedding of one skin for another, a process that demanded resilience, adaptability, and a profound well of emotional fortitude they may have underestimated.

Amina felt a profound sense of betrayal – not by Kayode, not by their new country, but by the illusion itself. Had she been sold a lie and bought it hook, line, and sinker? The narrative of 'Japa' was powerful, seductive, and deeply ingrained in the collective consciousness of those yearning for a better future. It promised an escape, a transcendence, a life where limitations dissolved. But what if the limitations weren't escaping, but merely changing form? What if the struggles they faced in Nigeria, while different, were replaced by an equally, if not more, insidious set of challenges here?

The exhaustion wasn't just physical; it was spiritual. It was the exhaustion of constantly performing, of trying to fit into a mould that felt alien. It was the weariness of bearing the family's emotional weight, of projecting an image of stability and control when, deep down, she felt she was constantly treading water. Kayode's own weariness mirrored hers, a silent testament to the toll this grand experiment was taking on them both.

The resentment, a dark, uninvited guest, had begun to fester. It was not about one person but about the situation, about the grand deception. She felt some guilt about this resentment, because she knew Kayode was doing his best and that he, too, was a victim of the pervasive narrative. Yet the feeling persisted, a bitter aftertaste to the supposed sweetness of their new life. She found herself replaying conversations, dissecting Kayode's words, searching for confirmation of her growing unease. Had he ever truly believed in the illusion? Or had he, like her, been swept up in the collective momentum, the desperate hope for something more?

She looked at their children's drawings pinned to the fridge – bright, colourful depictions of their new life, their school, their new friends. But Amina saw beyond the vibrant crayon strokes. She saw the forced smiles, the carefully constructed narratives of happiness that her children were already beginning to internalise. Were they happy, or simply good at pretending? The thought was a physical blow. She had wanted them to thrive, not just survive. She had wanted them to bloom, not just adapt.

The 'Japa' dream, in its purest form, was about opportunity. But opportunity, she was learning, was multifaceted. It wasn't just about economic advancement; it was about the chance to live a full, connected, emotionally rich life. And that was the very opportunity that seemed to be slipping through their fingers, like grains of sand. The constant striving, the relentless focus on the material, was creating a void, a space where genuine human connection and emotional nourishment should be.

She closed her eyes for a moment, letting the hum of the refrigerator wash over her. It was a sound that once signified progress, a symbol of their ability to afford such modern conveniences. Now it was a reminder of the sterile, controlled environment they inhabited, one that felt increasingly devoid of the warmth and spontaneity that had defined their lives back home. The promise had tarnished, revealing a landscape of exhaustion, isolation, and profound disillusionment. It was not just a chapter of hardship; it was a chapter of confrontation, a stark acknowledgement that the dream, as they had understood it, had been an illusion, a carefully constructed facade that was now beginning to crumble. And Amina, standing at the height of this crumbling edifice, knew that the most challenging part was yet to come, rebuilding not just a life but a new understanding of what success truly meant.

THE WEIGHT OF RESPONSIBILITY

Kayode found himself scrutinising the steady buzz from their refrigerator, as if the machine itself held the answers to his escalating unease. He was the provider, the protector, the architect of this London life. It was the role he had embraced with fierce, unwavering commitment, the mantle he had donned with pride. He had pictured himself as a determined oak, providing shade and shelter against the storms of uncertainty that had battered their lives in Nigeria. He had envisioned a family flourishing beneath his care, their laughter a vibrant chorus echoing through a secure, prosperous future.

But reality, as it so often did, had deviated sharply from the blueprint. The 'Japa' dream, the meticulously crafted narrative of upward mobility, had been built on a foundation of perceived necessity, a desperate scramble for a better tomorrow. And he, Kayode, had been the chief engineer of that scramble. He had poured his energy, intellect, and very being into securing their financial future, believing that material security was the bedrock of happiness. He had worked late nights, sacrificed weekends, and swallowed his fatigue and loneliness, all in pursuit of that glittering prize. He had believed, with almost religious fervour, that if he could provide enough, if he could shield them from the daily anxieties of bills and scarcity, then happiness would naturally follow.

Yet, watching Amina across the dinner table, a hollow ache spread through his chest. The spark that had once animated her eyes and the effortless grace with which she navigated their shared life seemed to have dimmed. Her silences were no longer companionable pauses but vast, uncharted territories. He saw the subtle tightening of her jaw when certain topics arose, and the way she steered conversations away from their past, as if harbouring a secret burden, he was not privy to or perhaps could not comprehend.

Her transformation from the vibrant, hopeful woman who had embraced him at Heathrow to this more reserved, often distant figure was a constant, unspoken question mark hanging over their lives. He had attributed her quietness to the inherent stress of relocation and the demanding adjustments of a new environment. But now a more unsettling possibility began to dawn: had his efforts to secure their future inadvertently stripped away something vital from their present? Had his unwavering focus on the material come at the expense of the emotional, the intangible, the very essence of their connection?

The weight of his responsibility felt heavier than ever, a physical burden settling on his shoulders and tightening his chest. He looked at his children, Kofi and Maya, their faces illuminated by the soft glow of the television, their attention caught by the cartoon's exaggerated antics. They were, in many ways, the epitome of the 'Japa' success story, adapting with remarkable ease to their new school, language, and friends. They spoke with British accents that, just a few years ago, had seemed impossibly distant.

They navigated the playground's complex social hierarchies with a confidence he envied. But beneath their outward adaptation, he detected a subtle undercurrent of something missing, a quiet yearning he couldn't quite define. He saw it in the way Maya sometimes paused, her eyes distant, as if searching for a lost memory. He heard it in Kofi's occasional thoughtful mentions of cousins and their laughter, a stark contrast to the more individualistic nature of their current friendships. He had wanted them to have opportunities, yes, but he had also wanted them to retain their joy, their uninhibited exuberance, the easy warmth that had characterised their childhood back home. He had provided them with safety and access to better education, but had he, in his relentless pursuit of these tangible benefits, inadvertently starved them of something equally crucial – the unburdened freedom of childhood he knew?

The financial pressures, while mitigated by his diligent efforts, remained a constant presence beneath the surface of their lives. The cost of living in London was a beast that demanded perpetual appeasement, and while he met its demands, it left little room for indulgence, for the spontaneous joys that had once punctuated their lives. He had secured them a comfortable, safe home. Still, it felt increasingly like a golden cage, its walls built with the bricks of sacrifice, and its windows offering only carefully curated views of a life perpetually out of reach. He yearned for the boisterous, chaotic warmth of family gatherings, the easy company of shared meals, and the comforting presence of a wider support network. Here, interactions were scheduled and social lives meticulously planned, a stark contrast to the organic nature of their former community. He missed the spontaneous laughter that had once filled their home and the comforting rhythm of everyday life, woven with the presence of loved ones.

He questioned his decision, the very bedrock of their new existence. Had he made the right choice for his family? The question, once a fleeting whisper, had become a relentless roar, echoing in the quiet hours of the night, mocking his carefully constructed rationale. He had believed, with every fibre of his being, that he was acting in their best interests, that he was setting them on a path to a brighter future. But the evidence, in the form of Amina's veiled anxieties and the children's subtle depression, suggested otherwise. He had aimed to be their protector and provider, and in doing so, he feared he had inadvertently alienated them from the very essence of what it meant to be a family. He had provided them with a different life, but had he robbed them of their own?

The pressure to maintain the facade of success and unwavering contentment was immense. Kayode saw it in Amina's carefully chosen words and polite smiles that didn't quite reach her eyes. He felt it in his own forced optimism and the rapid reassurances he offered when his doubts threatened to overwhelm him. Now trapped in a narrative he had helped create, one that demanded a constant performance of well-being, even when his soul felt deeply unsettled. He had sought to escape one set of anxieties, only to find himself ensnared by a new, more insidious set. The struggle was no longer about financial survival but about preserving their emotional core, the intangible threads that bound them together as a family.

He found himself envying the simplicity of the tasks he used to perform back home, the tangible satisfaction of seeing the direct impact of his efforts. Here, his work, while financially rewarding, felt abstract and disconnected from the everyday realities of his family's lives. He dealt in spreadsheets and deadlines, in abstract goals and projections, while Amina navigated the more immediate, emotional landscape of their home. He had provided the resources, but he had failed to provide the presence, the active engagement that fostered genuine connection. He had built them a fortress, but it was a fortress devoid of the warmth of shared experience, the comfort of unreserved intimacy.

The sacrifices he had made, the years of relentless effort, now felt like a heavy cloak, weighing him down rather than shielding him. He had envisioned a triumphant arrival, a moment of shared celebration and earned peace. Instead, he found himself in a quiet, internal battle, grappling with the realisation that the very foundations of his purpose, his identity as a provider and protector, were being challenged.

He had pursued a dream that was, perhaps, too narrowly defined, one that prioritised the external markers of success over the internal landscape of his family's well-being. As the weight of this realisation settled upon him, a profound sense of uncertainty about the future and his role within it took root. He had brought them to a new land, but in doing so he feared he had lost sight of what truly mattered on the journey: the shared experience, the emotional nourishment, the simple, profound act of being truly present for the ones he loved. The responsibility, he now understood, was not merely about providing for them but about nurturing them, about being the anchor that kept them grounded in their shared humanity, even as they navigated the currents of a new world.

SEEKING SOLUTION AMIDST CHAOS

The unease that had settled in Kayode's gut was no longer a whisper; it was a persistent drumbeat, demanding his attention. He couldn't afford to drift in a sea of introspection, not when the very fabric of his family felt so precariously frayed. The carefully constructed edifice of their London life, the dream he had so enthusiastically pursued, was showing cracks, and he knew, with a certainty that chilled him, that inaction would lead to its eventual collapse. The weight of his responsibility, once a source of pride, now felt like an anchor dragging him down. He had always been a man of action, a problem-solver, and the current predicament demanded nothing less.

His first instinct was to turn to the wisdom of those who had walked this path before him. The Nigerian community in London, though dispersed and often struggling in their own ways, offered the practical advice he hoped for. He remembered the informal gatherings, the weekend get-togethers where stories of hardship and triumph were exchanged over bowls of jollof rice and platters of fried plantain. These were not formal institutions, but organic networks of support built on shared heritage and mutual understanding. He thought of Elder Adebayo, a man whose quiet dignity and measured pronouncements had always commanded respect. Elder Adebayo had arrived in the UK decades ago, navigating the choppy waters of immigration with a resilience that Kayode now desperately needed to emulate.

He decided to reach out. A phone call led to an invitation to Elder Adebayo's modest home in East London. The journey felt longer than usual, each mile a testament to the widening rift between his aspirations and his current reality. When he finally arrived, he was warmly received, easing some of the tension in his shoulders. Elder Adebayo's living room was a testament to a life lived with purpose, filled with family photographs, worn books, and the comforting aroma of brewing tea.

As Kayode recounted his story, carefully omitting the more painful parts of his marital discord but focusing on the overarching sense of disconnect and the fear of failure, Elder Adebayo listened with attentive stillness. He didn't interrupt, but his wise, compassionate eyes conveyed deep understanding. When Kayode finally fell silent, the silence stretched, not uncomfortably but thoughtfully.

"Kayode," Elder Adebayo began, his voice a low rumble, "the 'Japa' journey is a steep climb. Many reach the summit only to realise the view is not what they imagined. We come seeking a better life, yes, but sometimes we forget that 'better' is not always measured in pounds and pence. It is measured in laughter, in connection, in the peace of knowing your loved ones are truly at ease." He paused, taking a slow sip of his tea. "You have built a strong house, Kayode, brick by brick. But a house is more than its walls. It is the warmth within, the shared meals, the stories told in the quiet hours. You have provided the shelter, but have you lit the fire?"

Elder Adebayo emphasised the importance of intentional community and of carving out spaces for genuine connection amid the relentless demands of earning a living. He shared anecdotes about his own struggles, including the early days when loneliness was a constant companion, and how he had found solace and strength only by actively seeking out and building relationships with fellow Nigerians. He advised Kayode to participate actively in community events, volunteer his time, and offer his skills not just for financial gain but for the sheer joy of contributing and connecting. "Let your children see you not just as the provider, but as a man who is part of something larger than himself," he counselled. "Let them see the richness that comes from giving, from being a thread in the tapestry of our community."

He also touched on the delicate art of communication, particularly with Amina. "Amina," he said, his gaze steady, "she carries her own burdens. I am sure of it. A wife who feels unheard and unseen can grow weary. You must find a way to speak her language, Kayode. Not just the language of bills and futures, but the language of the heart. Find the quiet moments, the shared glances, and speak from that place. It is often in the unspoken understanding that the deepest connections happen, but sometimes the unspoken needs a voice."

As Kayode left Elder Adebayo's home, he felt a renewed sense of purpose, though tinged with the daunting realisation of the work ahead. The elder's words resonated deeply, echoing the unspoken anxieties that had been agitating him. He had been so focused on the destination, on the tangible markers of success, that he had neglected the journey, the vital, shared experience of building a life together.

Beyond seeking counsel, Kayode recognised the need for a more structured approach to their finances. While he had managed to keep them afloat, the constant pressure was undoubtedly a contributing factor to the underlying tension. He decided to explore financial counselling services specifically for immigrant families. He had heard of organisations that offered guidance on budgeting, debt management, and even investment strategies tailored to the unique challenges newcomers face. He understood that this wasn't about admitting failure but about gaining a clearer perspective and developing a more sustainable strategy for their long-term financial well-being. He needed to ensure that their pursuit of economic security wasn't inadvertently jeopardising their emotional security.

The thought of confronting Amina directly with his feelings, however, remained a formidable hurdle. Their communication had become a delicate dance, a series of polite exchanges that skirted the deeper issues. He feared that a direct approach might provoke defensiveness or, worse, a quiet withdrawal that would further entrench the distance between them. Yet he knew he couldn't continue living in this state of polite estrangement. He began to contemplate small, deliberate acts of connection. Perhaps it would be a shared cup of tea in the morning, a moment to be present without the pressure of conversation. Or possibly a weekend outing, not a grand gesture but something simple and shared, like a walk in a park they hadn't visited before, a space to create new, shared memories. He resolved to try to initiate conversations that focused on their shared past, the happy moments they had experienced together, in the hope of rekindling that lost spark. He would start by recalling their early days, the dreams they had shared before the 'Japa' imperative had taken hold, trying to remind them of the foundation upon which their love stood.

He also considered the impact of his own behaviour. Had his relentless focus on work, long hours, and often-preoccupied disposition contributed to Amina's sense of isolation? He began to make a conscious effort to be more present at home. He put away his work laptop during dinner, made a point of engaging with the children in their activities, and actively sought opportunities to spend time with Amina, even if it was just watching a film together or sharing a quiet evening. These were small steps, perhaps, but he believed that consistent, intentional effort could slowly begin to mend the rifts that had formed.

Kayode also turned his thoughts to his children, Maya and Kofi. Their adaptation, while outwardly impressive, had also been a source of quiet concern. He wanted them to embrace their new lives without losing their Nigerian heritage, their roots. He decided to actively seek out cultural events, Nigerian festivals, and even language classes to help him reconnect with his identity. He remembered the vibrant energy of their childhood back home, the music, the stories, the sense of belonging. He wanted to recreate that sense of cultural richness here, to ensure they grew up with a strong sense of who they were, wherever they lived. He began researching local Nigerian cultural centres and community groups, eager to find ways to immerse his children in the traditions integral to their identity.

The path ahead was undeniably challenging. The emotional complexities of their situation remained tangled, and the financial pressures, though addressed, remained a reality. But Kayode felt a flicker of hope, rekindled by his conversations and renewed determination.

He was no longer content to watch the disintegration of his family life passively. He was an architect, and while the initial blueprints had proven flawed, he was still capable of renovating, rebuilding, and finding new solutions amidst the chaos. The dream was not dead, he realised. Still, it had to be redefined, reshaped to encompass not just material prosperity but also the intangible wealth of a connected, loving, and contented family. It was his new mission; he prepared to fight for it, one deliberate, courageous step at a time.

He understood that the size of his bank account would not measure true success, but by the strength of the bonds he managed to preserve and nurture. This stark and profound realisation became his guiding star on the turbulent journey ahead.

THE EROSION OF PARTNERSHIP

The echo of Elder Adebayo's words, "Have you nurtured the fireplace?", reverberated in Kayode's mind, a gentle yet persistent accusation. It wasn't just about the physical structure of their London life, the comfortable house in a decent neighbourhood, the children attending good schools – those were the outward manifestations of a dream. The fireplace, he now understood with a clarity that was both heartbreaking and illuminating, was the warmth, the unspoken understanding, the shared rhythm of their lives that had once pulsed between him and Amina. And that heart, he had to admit, had grown cold.

He found himself replaying conversations, not the arguments, but the quiet moments, the stolen glances, the easy silences that spoke volumes. He remembered their early days in London, the cramped flat they had first shared, where money was even scarcer but laughter seemed to flow more freely. Amina had been a whirlwind of supportive energy then, his fiercest cheerleader, her belief in him a force that had sustained him through countless setbacks. They had navigated the initial shock of a new country, the alien sounds and smells, the bureaucracy that seemed designed to confound, together. They had been a unit, a two-person army against the world, their shared struggles forging a bond that felt unbreakable.

He recalled a particular evening, barely a year after their arrival. A particularly demoralising job rejection had left him feeling deflated, questioning his decision to uproot their lives.

Amina found him staring out of their rain-streaked window, the grey London sky mirroring his mood. She hadn't offered platitudes or false reassurances. Instead, she had sat beside him, taken his hand, and begun to hum a tune from home, a familiar folk song that evoked memories of shared joy and resilience. Then she began to speak, not about the job but about their dreams, the vision they had for their future here, and the sacrifices they were making for their children. She reminded him of the fierce pride they felt when they finally secured their first proper apartment, and of the delight in their children's excited chatter as they discovered new parks and playgrounds. It wasn't about dismissing his disappointment, but about reframing it, about reminding him of the strength they possessed when they faced challenges together. That night, they talked for hours, not about problems but about their shared aspirations, their love for each other, and their unwavering commitment to building a life that was more than just survival. It was a reaffirmation, a quiet, powerful declaration of their partnership.

Where had Amina gone? Or, more honestly, where had they gone? The question was now a constant companion. He saw the shift not as a sudden disaster but as a slow, insidious erosion. It began subtly, with the increasing demands of his work, the longer hours, and the mental space consumed by the relentless pursuit of financial security. Amina, too, was working, juggling her own job, the demands of motherhood, and the upkeep of their home. But the nature of their contributions had somehow shifted. He became the primary provider, the one who bore the financial burden, and, with that, he felt, came a subtle shift in their dynamic. His responsibilities grew, and with them came a sense of self-imposed isolation. He was the problem-solver, the shield, the one who had to make the tough decisions.

He remembered a heated discussion about the children's extracurricular activities. Amina had wanted Kofi to join the local football team, seeing it as a vital way for him to integrate and make friends. Kayode, however, had hesitated over the cost, the extra travel time, and the perceived distraction from his studies. He had argued with a logic that felt irrefutable to him at the time – that their priority had to be academic success, securing their future. Amina had pleaded, her voice tinged with frustration, "Kayode, he needs to be a child, not just a student! He needs to feel like he belongs here and not processed." He had dismissed her concerns as emotional overreactions, a failure to grasp the long-term strategy. In his mind, he was being pragmatic; in hers, he was being rigid, unfeeling, and dismissive of her understanding of their son's needs. That was the moment, he now realised, when their shared vision began to diverge. He focused on the destination, the abstract idea of future success, while she was acutely aware of the present, the emotional landscape of their family.

The resentment, he saw now, was a slow-acting poison. It wasn't born of malice but of unmet needs and unspoken frustrations that festered. He felt a pang of guilt as he replayed his own contributions to this decay. He had become so consumed by external pressures that he had stopped investing in the internal engine of their relationship. He had expected Amina to understand his sacrifices and appreciate his efforts without needing to voice them. He had fallen into the trap of believing that providing for the family was the sole measure of his worth as a husband and partner.

He had forgotten that partnership was a reciprocal dance, a continuous exchange of support, understanding, and emotional intimacy.

He had stopped truly listening. He would hear Amina's words, but his mind would be miles away, planning the next move in his relentless quest for stability. He'd nod, offer a perfunctory response, and then return to his own internal monologue. He had mistaken silence for contentment, or worse, for acceptance. He hadn't recognised the subtle cues, the weariness in her voice, the way her eyes would sometimes drift away when he spoke, as if she were no longer present in the conversation. He had been so busy building the house that he had forgotten to inhabit it with her, to share its joys and its burdens in equal measure.

The physical intimacy had dwindled too, replaced by a polite, almost mechanical affection. Kayode remembered the early days when touch was an instinctive expression of their connection, a spontaneous gesture of love and comfort. Now it felt forced, often initiated by him out of a sense of obligation rather than desire. He saw the flicker of resignation in her eyes when he reached for her, the subtle withdrawal that spoke volumes about the emotional distance that had grown between them. He had become so focused on the external manifestations of success – the job, the house, the children's achievements – that he had neglected the very foundation of their partnership. This emotional and intimate connection had once defined their marriage.

He had often thought of their partnership as a durable bridge, built to withstand life's storms. But bridges, he now understood, required constant maintenance. Without regular inspection and reinforcement, the foundations could weaken, the structure could be compromised, and eventually it could buckle under its own weight. He had allowed the bridge to stand untended, assuming its strength was immutable. He had failed to recognise the subtle tremors, the hairline cracks that had begun to appear, and instead he had focused on the distant horizon, on the promised land of financial security.

The pain of this realisation was an ache in his chest. It wasn't the sharp sting of betrayal or the fiery anger of a fight. It was a profound sadness, a mourning for something precious lost, not through external forces but through his own neglect. He felt a deep sense of responsibility, recognising that he, too, had played a significant role in the erosion of their shared vision. He had become so adept at navigating the external world and solving practical problems that he had become blind to the internal landscape of his marriage, the delicate ecosystem of their emotional connection.

He thought of Amina's quiet strength and her resilience in the face of his frequent preoccupations. She had carried so much, silently and without complaint, for so long. He had interpreted her patience as a sign of her contentment, a reflection of her ability to adapt and thrive. But now he saw it for what it truly was: a testament to her enduring love, a quiet hope that he would eventually see what he was missing and bridge the gap that had opened between them. He had mistaken her patience for an unlimited resource, and in doing so he had placed an immense burden upon it.

The question that haunted him was not whether their partnership had eroded, but how he had allowed it to happen. He sifted through memories, searching for definitive moments, for the tipping points that had led them to this place of quiet desperation. He saw his own ambition, once a driving force for their collective good, morph into a singular obsession. He saw his tendency to retreat into his own thoughts when stressed, a habit that had prevented him from sharing his vulnerabilities with Amina, thereby denying her the chance to support him and strengthen their bond. He saw his assumption that his way was the right way, a subtle arrogance that had silenced her voice and diminished her contributions.

He now understood that the 'Japa' journey, while promising a better future, had also demanded a toll. It had stretched their resources, time, and emotional reserves to the breaking point. In the scramble to survive and thrive in a new environment, the art of maintaining a partnership had been an unintended casualty. He had been so focused on the tangible, on building a secure future for his family, that he had neglected the intangible, the emotional glue that held them together.

The dream they had once shared had become his dream, and he had, inadvertently, expected Amina to follow in its wake rather than actively co-create it with him. The partnership, once a vibrant, living entity, had been reduced to a functional arrangement, a necessary component of their shared existence, but devoid of its former passion and shared purpose. This realisation was not a comfortable one; it was a reckoning, a stark confrontation with his own role in the slow, quiet dissolution of the most crucial partnership of his life. He knew, with a certainty that settled deep in his bones, that he could not afford to let this continue. The journey back, he suspected, would be far more arduous than the journey here.

A NEW DEFINITION OF HOME

The rain, a constant companion in this adopted land, drummed a monotonous rhythm against the windowpane. It was a sound Kayode had once found almost comforting, a gentle song in the early days of their London sojourn. Now it felt like a mournful song, a soundtrack to his introspection. He looked around their comfortable semi-detached house, a testament to years of relentless effort, of sacrificed comforts and deferred dreams. The polished furniture gleamed under the soft lamplight, the shelves were organised, and their children's artwork was proudly displayed on the refrigerator door. By all outward appearances, they had built a life. They had achieved the 'success' that had seemed so elusive back home, the kind that was measured in square footage, in school reports, and in the absence of overt financial worry. Yet the word 'home' felt like a ghost, a pain for something that was no longer truly there.

He'd always equated 'home' with the physical space they inhabited and the tangible markers of a life well-lived. Back in Nigeria, 'home' had been the bustling compound, shared meals, and the loudness of voices that blended into a sense of belonging. It had been the scent of his mother's cooking, the warmth of familiar sunlight, and the easy company of extended family. Here, in London, 'home' had initially been the cramped flat, filled with the scent of optimism and Amina's unshakeable faith. It had been the shared struggle, whispered hopes in the dead of night, and the fierce protectiveness they felt for each other against the vast indifference of a new world. They had poured their essence into this physical structure, believing that by mastering the external they could secure their internal world. But the foundation, he now realised, had been laid on shifting sand.

The concept of 'home' had, for him, become inextricably linked to the 'Japa' narrative, the great migration in pursuit of a better future. It was a journey, a destination, a grand achievement. But the journey itself had demanded a price, a slow, almost gradual amputation of the very things that made a place feel like home. He saw it now not as a dramatic rupture but as a gradual unravelling. The relentless drive to provide had become an all-consuming quest for financial security. He had been so focused on building the fortress that he had forgotten to cultivate the garden within its walls. The emotional landscape, the nurturing of their shared life, had been relegated to the periphery, a secondary concern to address after the real work.

He recalled the words of an elder, a gentle admonishment about the importance of 'nurturing the fireplace'. At the time, he had interpreted it in a purely pragmatic sense – ensuring the house was warm and the bills were paid. He hadn't grasped the deeper, more profound meaning. The fireplace wasn't just about physical warmth; it was about the warmth of connection, the shared glow of intimacy and understanding. It was the embers of their shared past that should have been tended, fanned by shared laughter and whispered confessions, not left to die out in the relentless wind of his ambition. He had been so busy ensuring their physical shelter from the storm that he had allowed the internal atmosphere to grow cold.

This new understanding was disorienting, like looking at a familiar landscape through a distorted lens. The London skyline, once a symbol of aspiration, now seemed stark and impersonal. The meticulously manicured gardens, the orderly streets, the polite but distant interactions – all contributed to a sense of being an observer rather than a participant in the life they had painstakingly constructed. He had achieved the outward signs of belonging, but the inner resonance, the deep-seated feeling of being truly at home, remained elusive. It was a homesickness not for a geographical location but for a state of being, for the emotional equilibrium that had once defined their family.

He thought of their children, Maya and Kofi. They were not born here, but their memories had soaked up the rhythm of London life. They spoke with impeccable English accents, their tastes shaped by the cultural currents of this land. Yet he saw in them, too, a certain detachment, a subtle longing for something they couldn't quite articulate. Were they, too, caught in this nebulous definition of home? Had their upbringing, so focused on academic and material achievement, inadvertently created a generation of children who were excellent at navigating the external world but disconnected from the internal landscape of their own family? He had striven to give them the best of both worlds, but he was beginning to fear he had given them neither. They lived in a comfortable house and attended good schools, but were they truly rooted? Did they possess that unshakeable sense of belonging, that innate understanding of where they came from, that had always anchored him, even in his most challenging moments?

The truth, he admitted to himself, was that he had equated his own success with his family's well-being. He had believed that by providing them with material security and shielding them from the financial anxieties that had marked his own youth, he was fulfilling his role as a father and husband. But he had overlooked the fundamental truth: that true provision extends far beyond the tangible. It encompasses emotional availability, shared experiences, and the unwavering presence of a united partnership. The act of providing consumed him, and he had neglected the art of being present.

This shift was not sudden but gradual, like the slow emergence of the sun on a cloudy morning. It was a reckoning with the consequences of his choices, a stark acknowledgement of the unintended casualties of his ambition. He began to understand that the 'Japa' journey, while it had undoubtedly opened doors and offered opportunities, had also demanded a renegotiation of their fundamental understanding of 'home'. It wasn't simply a matter of transplanting their lives to new soil; it was about cultivating a new garden, one that required not just the right soil and sunlight but also consistent watering, careful weeding, and a deep, abiding connection to the roots from which it sprang.

He realised that his definition of success had been too narrow, too focused on external metrics. True success, he now understood, was a more holistic concept, encompassing his family's emotional health, the strength of his marriage, and his own inner peace. It was about the quality of their shared lives, not just the quantity of their possessions. This wasn't to say financial stability was unimportant; it was the bedrock on which everything else had been built. But it was not, and could never be, the entirety of the structure.

The journey back to a sense of home, he suspected, would be far more challenging than the one that had brought him here. It would require him to dismantle some of the carefully constructed walls he had built around himself, expose his vulnerabilities, and re-engage with Amina on a deeper, more authentic level. It would mean admitting that his relentless focus on the future had come at the expense of their present and of priceless moments of shared intimacy and connection, which he had sacrificed on the altar of his ambition.

He looked at Amina, sitting across the room, engrossed in a book. He saw the lines of weariness around her eyes, the subtle slump of her shoulders that spoke of a burden carried for too long. He had mistaken her quiet resilience for acceptance, her patience for contentment. He hadn't seen the slow erosion of her spirit, the quiet resignation that had begun to settle in. He had been too preoccupied with the external battle for survival to notice the quietening of his own home.

The rain had softened to a drizzle, and a sliver of moon had appeared between the clouds. Kayode rose and walked to the window, his gaze fixed on the patch of sky. 'Home,' he murmured to himself, the word tasting foreign yet familiar on his tongue. It was no longer just a place. It was a feeling, a connection, a shared narrative. It was the fireplace that needed rekindling, not with the dry twigs of ambition, but with shared love and understanding.

The journey back to that fireplace, he knew, would be the most critical he would ever undertake. It was not a journey of miles, but of moments, of rediscovered intimacy, and of a profound, perhaps painful, redefinition of what it truly meant to be home. He had to find his way back, not just for himself, but for Amina, for Kofi, for Maya, and for the spirit of the family so inadvertently fractured in the pursuit of a brighter future. The dream, he now understood, was not just about having a better life, but about living a better life together. That began with rediscovering the lost warmth of their fireplace and redefining 'home' not as a destination, but as a sanctuary of the heart. It was not merely a philosophical contemplation; it was a blueprint for his future, a guide for his reckoning. He had to learn to build not just a life, but a home, from the inside out. The external fortress was strong, but the internal dwelling needed urgent renovation, deep soul-searching, and restoration.

CHAPTER 9

THE PROMISES, PAYOFFS & UNFOLDING FUTURE

THE LINGERING PROMISE

The rain had ceased, leaving crisp, clean air that carried the faint scents of damp earth and blooming jasmine from Mrs Higgins' Garden next door. Kayode stood by the window, his fingers tracing the condensation patterns left by his breath. He'd lost himself in thought for what felt like hours, the echoes of his earlier introspection still resonating within him. But now a different kind of thought settled in, one that looked forward, not backward. The promise. That was the word that resurfaced, not as a faded inscription on a forgotten tablet, but as a vibrant, living thing. The promise of a better future for Kofi and Maya. It was the bedrock upon which they migrated and the beacon that had guided them through the roughest seas.

He watched Maya, now a teenager, hunched over her laptop in the living room, her brow furrowed in concentration as she navigated the complex terrain of a coding tutorial. The sheer focus radiating from her was a testament to her inherent drive, a spark Kayode recognised and deeply admired. It wasn't just about rote learning; it was about genuine curiosity and a desire to understand and master. Back home, such opportunities would have been a luxury, a privilege reserved for a select few. Here, they were, for the most part, accessible. The resources available to Maya – the online courses, the coding clubs at school, the sheer breadth of information at her fingertips – were precisely what Kayode had envisioned when they first dreamed of a life in the UK. It was a tangible manifestation of the promise, a quiet but powerful affirmation that their sacrifices had not been in vain.

Kofi was now looking lanky. His energetic spirit was channelled into his violin practice, the slightly wavering notes filling the house with a determined melody. He practised with an intensity that belied his years, each hesitant phrase gradually yielding to a more confident flow. He remembered the hesitant discussions about extracurricular activities, the initial concerns about the cost of lessons, and the instrument itself. But Amina, ever the pragmatist, had found a way, enrolling Kofi in a community music programme that offered subsidised lessons. Seeing Kofi's face light up with pride after a particularly successful practice session, or witnessing his collaborative spirit during ensemble rehearsals, filled Kayode with quiet joy. It was more than just learning an instrument; it was about fostering discipline, the joy of creation, and building confidence and social skills in a diverse environment. These were the subtle yet profound elements of the promise he had almost overlooked in his obsession with financial metrics.

He now understood that the promise wasn't solely about escaping hardship or achieving material wealth. It was about creating an environment where their children could explore their potential and have their innate talents nurtured and allowed to blossom. It was about access to a broader world of ideas, cultures, and opportunities that might have remained forever out of reach in their homeland. The challenges they had faced – the initial struggles with the language, the cultural nuances that sometimes felt like an impenetrable fog, the constant worry of homesickness – were all part of the price. But the return, Kayode was beginning to see, was immeasurable.

He recalled a recent conversation with Maya about her aspirations. Maya spoke with a passion that surprised Kayode, detailing her desire to work in artificial intelligence and contribute to technological advances that could, in turn, benefit their home country. It wasn't the vague ambition of a child; it was a considered, informed goal, shaped by the education and exposure she was receiving. This was the payoff, not in pounds and pence, but in the forging of young minds, equipped with the tools and vision to make a difference. Kayode had always wanted his children to be successful in the conventional sense, to have stable jobs and comfortable lives. But hearing Maya speak of contributing to society's betterment, of using her skills to create positive change, was a far greater reward than any he had dared to imagine.

Kofi, too, was developing a quiet strength. He navigated the complexities of friendships with a grace that Kayode envied, learning to compromise, empathise and stand up for himself. His school offered a broader curriculum, exposing him to subjects not typically part of the Nigerian educational system, which ignited a passion for geography, music, and literature that delighted Kayode. He saw him not just as his son but as a young man at the point of discovering his own voice and unique perspective on the world. This was the unfolding future, the tangible evidence that the leap of faith they had taken years ago was indeed yielding fruit.

It wasn't a fairy tale, of course. He knew the hurdles still ahead for Maya and Kofi. The competitive nature of higher education, the challenges of finding meaningful employment in a globalised economy, and the ongoing need to navigate their dual identities. There would be moments of disappointment, setbacks, and doubt. But the resilience he witnessed in them, the sheer determination they displayed, gave him immense hope. They were not passive recipients of opportunity; they were active participants, shaping their own destinies within the framework Kayode and Amina had painstakingly helped to construct.

He thought of the children of his friends back home who had stayed. Their stories were varied, some undoubtedly happy, others touched by the regret of missed chances. He didn't for a moment believe that a life lived in Nigeria would have been inherently worse. It would have been different, undoubtedly richer in some cultural respects, perhaps. But for Maya and Kofi, given their specific aptitudes and the paths they seemed destined to forge, this was the right place. The diversity of experiences available to them here, the exposure to different ways of thinking, the sheer breadth of cultural exchange – these were the intangible assets that formed a crucial part of the promise. They were learning to be global citizens, not just Nigerians living abroad.

The initial anxieties, the fear of the unknown, had begun to recede, replaced by a steady, albeit sometimes shaky, confidence. Kayode knew that the challenges he grappled with in his own journey – the sense of being an outsider, subtle prejudices, and the struggle for recognition – were, in some ways, preparing Maya and Kofi. They were learning to be adaptable and open-minded, and to understand that the world was a complex tapestry of different peoples and perspectives. They were developing a thicker skin, yes, but also a more balanced understanding of humanity.

This renewed appreciation for the promise didn't erase the pain of what was lost or the emotional disconnect he had been feeling. But it provided a vital counterbalance. It was a reminder that the Japa journey, with all its arduous demands, had also been a journey of profound opportunity for his children. He looked at Maya again, a small smile playing on her lips as she finally cracked a complex code. Kayode knew the real payoff wasn't just in Maya's future career, but in the sheer satisfaction of intellectual conquest and the quiet triumph of perseverance. And Kofi, his violin now producing a clear, resonant note, was not just practising scales; he was weaving his own story, note by note.

The promise, once a distant star, was now a constellation, its brilliance illuminating the path ahead, not just for his children but for him too, as he continued to navigate the complex and often surprising landscape of their new home. The future, once a vague dream, was solidifying, taking shape in the determined focus of his daughter and the budding creativity of his son. This was the true payoff, a legacy being built not just on material success but on the thriving spirits of the next generation.

NEGOTIATING THE NEW REALITIES

The sound of domesticity had shifted, evolving from the frantic scramble for survival to a more settled, albeit still evolving, rhythm. The early days, a blur of anxiety and relentless effort, had gradually given way to a state Kayode tentatively labelled 'equilibrium'. It wasn't a return to the ease and familiarity of their former life, nor was it the golden utopia they had perhaps naively envisioned. Instead, it was a landscape of negotiation, a constant recalibration of roles, expectations, and even desires. The dream, once a singular, brilliant point, had fragmented, its rays scattering to illuminate their reality.

Amina, her hands busy with the evening meal, had initiated many of these subtle adjustments. The initial unspoken agreement, a silent pact forged in the vacuum of their migration, had been about shared sacrifice. Now, as the immediate pressures eased, the unspoken began to require articulation. There were conversations about finances that were no longer about immediate survival but about future planning – university fees, potential investments, even the occasional indulgence that had seemed an unthinkable luxury just months before.

Kayode found himself less the sole architect of their financial security and more a participant in a shared stewardship. Amina meticulously tracked household expenses, and her uncanny ability to find the best deals on everything from groceries to school uniforms had always been the bedrock of their pragmatism. But now her input carried a weight that extended beyond mere pragmatism; it was about building a sustainable future, a shared vision for their life here. Their communication, once strained by sheer exhaustion, began to flow with a newfound ease. There were fewer accusations born of stress and more discussions born of mutual respect and a shared understanding of their progress.

He remembered one evening, after Kofi had aced a particularly challenging maths test, when he and Amina had sat in the quiet of their small living room, the faint murmur of the television providing a backdrop to their conversation. "We did it, Kayode," Amina had said, her voice soft yet firm. "We gave them this chance." It wasn't just about the academic achievement; it was about the environment that had fostered it. Access to resources, the quality of teaching, and the sheer breadth of opportunities available at Kofi's school – these were the elements Amina had always championed, and Kayode was now fully appreciating. He realised he had been so focused on the tangible markers of success, the job titles and salary figures, that he had sometimes overlooked the less quantifiable yet equally vital aspects of their progress.

This evolving understanding extended to their roles within the family unit. Kayode had always been the primary breadwinner, bearing the financial burden. Now, with his consultancy work gaining traction and Amina's part-time role at the local library blossoming into something more substantial, their contributions were becoming more balanced. It wasn't a simple exchange of roles, but a redefinition. Kayode still shouldered significant responsibility, but he also felt a greater freedom to pursue projects that truly ignited his passion, rather than those that paid the bills. Amina, in turn, found a renewed sense of purpose and professional identity, with her intelligence and organisational skills finally finding a broader canvas on which to express themselves. This shift had also had a ripple effect on the children. They saw not just parents, but individuals with evolving careers and a shared commitment to their family's well-being.

However, this new equilibrium wasn't entirely self-generated. After much deliberation and with Amina's characteristic foresight, she sought external support. A local immigrant support network, which they initially approached with apprehension, had become an invaluable resource. It offered not only practical advice on navigating the complexities of the UK's bureaucratic systems – tax codes, housing benefits, healthcare – but also a crucial sense of community. Meeting other families who had embarked on similar journeys and sharing stories of triumphs and setbacks had been a powerful antidote to the isolation that had often plagued Kayode. It was a reminder that they were not alone and that their struggles, while unique, were part of a larger narrative. He recalled a particular session on financial planning, where a speaker, herself a migrant who had built a successful business, shared practical strategies for managing income and expenses in the UK context. It was a revelation, demystifying aspects of personal finance that had previously seemed opaque and intimidating.

The initial shock of cultural difference, which had once felt like a constant, invisible barrier, had begun to recede, not through assimilation but through deeper understanding. Kayode and Amina had consciously tried to engage with their new environment, not just as observers but as active participants. They attended local community events, volunteered for school fundraisers, and even joined a book club that met at the local library. These interactions, often starting with awkward pleasantries, had gradually blossomed into genuine friendships. They were learning the unspoken rules, the cultural shorthand, the humour, and the shared values that underpinned British society, while also finding ways to maintain and share their own cultural heritage. It wasn't about abandoning their identity but about enriching it, about weaving their own threads into the broader tapestry of their adopted country.

The children, too, were finding their footing in this renegotiated reality. Maya, with her growing tech prowess, was increasingly engaging with the broader world through online communities and international coding competitions. She was learning to collaborate with people from diverse backgrounds, communicate across cultural divides, and present her work with confidence. Kofi, meanwhile, was not only excelling in his music but also finding his voice in school debates and student council activities. He was learning to articulate his opinions, negotiate different perspectives, and advocate for his beliefs.

Kayode realised that he had been so focused on providing them with opportunities that he hadn't fully appreciated the self-driven agency they were developing. They weren't just passive recipients of good fortune; they were active architects of their own futures, equipped with the skills and confidence to navigate the complexities of the world they were inheriting.

Yet the renegotiation was an ongoing process, a perpetual dance between the past and the present, the dream and the reality. There were still moments of doubt, flashes of homesickness, and the occasional sting of misunderstanding. The financial pressures, though lessened, still loomed as a constant reminder of the precariousness of their situation. But the crucial difference was that they faced these challenges together, armed with a deeper understanding of each other, a stronger sense of purpose, and a more profound appreciation for the promise that had brought them here.

That dream was not abandoned but transformed. It was no longer a singular, distant star but a constellation of individual points of light – academic success, personal growth, a sense of belonging, shared family strength – illuminating a path that, while still uncertain, was undeniably their own. They were not merely surviving; they were beginning to thrive, to truly inhabit their new reality, not as immigrants clinging to the fringes but as integral contributors to the vibrant, complex mosaic of their adopted home. The payoffs were no longer merely hypothetical future rewards; they were the everyday victories, the quiet moments of connection, the shared laughter that echoed through their home, a testament to a promise that, against all odds, was steadily unfolding.

The initial euphoria of arrival, the almost dizzying relief of having successfully navigated the treacherous waters of international relocation, had long since subsided. In its place, a more grounded yet equally profound sense of accomplishment was taking root. Kayode found himself reflecting on the subtle shifts within their family dynamic, a quiet evolution that spoke volumes about their adaptation to this new world. The frantic energy of survival, the constant vigilance required to keep their heads above water, had gradually been replaced by a more considered, deliberate pace of life. This wasn't a return to the unburdened ease of their past, but rather a conscious construction of a new kind of stability, one built not on familiarity but on understanding and a shared commitment to their future.

Amina, he observed, had become the silent architect of this new equilibrium. Her pragmatism, a quality he had always admired, now extended beyond the meticulous management of their household budget. It permeated their communication, transforming potentially fraught discussions into collaborative problem-solving sessions.

The anxieties that had once manifested as open dialogue had given way to hushed, late-night worries. They spoke about the children's futures with a clarity that surprised Kayode, no longer as abstract hopes but as tangible goals, each with a carefully considered plan of action. He recalled a recent conversation about Maya's university aspirations. It had begun with Kayode voicing his concerns about the exorbitant tuition fees, a familiar knot of anxiety tightening in his chest. But Amina, rather than succumbing to negativity, had calmly presented a detailed breakdown of potential scholarships, student loans, and part-time work opportunities, even identifying specific university courses that aligned with Kofi's emerging interests. It wasn't about dismissing his concerns; it was about confronting them with a practical, actionable strategy, a testament to their evolving partnership.

This collaborative approach extended to their individual roles within the family. Kayode's consultancy work, initially a desperate attempt to shore up their finances, had begun to flourish. He found himself increasingly sought after for his unique blend of industry experience and cross-cultural insight. This newfound professional satisfaction, coupled with Amina's growing confidence and responsibility in her role at the library, had subtly shifted the traditional power dynamics. It wasn't a dramatic upheaval, but a gentle redistribution of weight. Kayode still bore significant financial responsibility, but he no longer felt the crushing isolation of carrying it alone. He delegated tasks at work and at home, trusting Amina's judgment and appreciating her contributions more deeply. This mutual respect, in turn, fostered greater autonomy for both, allowing them to pursue their individual passions without compromising their shared vision.

The children, in many ways, were the living embodiment of this renegotiated reality. Maya's femininity had become more prominent. She was no longer merely a recipient of educational opportunities but an active explorer of them. Her expedition into coding had blossomed into a genuine passion, and she spent hours immersed in online forums, collaborating with peers from around the globe. Kayode found himself less guiding Maya and more learning from her, witnessing his daughter's innate ability to navigate complex digital landscapes with an ease that Kayode himself struggled to comprehend. This was the payoff, not in material terms but in the sight of his daughter confidently charting her own course, equipped with the tools and resilience to succeed in a world Kayode himself was still learning to understand.

Kofi, too, was blossoming. His lanky frame was filling out. His violin, once a source of tentative melodies, now filled their home with rich, resonant sounds. But his growth wasn't confined to the practice room. He had found his voice at school, actively participating, winning in music competitions, and performing in live concerts, including the annual all-high-school-band competition. His youthful naivety was now tempered by a growing understanding of the world's complexities. Seeing him articulate

his opinions with conviction, even when they differed from his own, filled Kayode with quiet pride.
This gradual integration into their new environment was facilitated by their willingness to seek out and embrace external support systems. The local community centre, initially visited out of necessity for language classes, had become a hub of social and practical assistance. They had forged friendships with other migrant families, sharing advice on everything from navigating the NHS to understanding the nuances of British school admissions.

These connections had provided a vital buffer against the isolation that could so easily creep in, reminding them that their journey, while unique, was part of a larger, shared human experience. Kayode particularly remembered a workshop on financial planning for new arrivals, where a speaker, herself a successful entrepreneur who had migrated years earlier, shared practical strategies for navigating the UK's economic landscape. It was a moment of profound clarity, demystifying aspects of banking, credit, and investment that had previously seemed daunting and inaccessible. This wasn't just about surviving; it was about thriving, about building a secure and prosperous future.

The initial cultural schisms, the moments of awkwardness and misunderstanding that had once felt like insurmountable barriers, were also beginning to soften. Through active engagement like attending local festivals, joining neighbourhood watch schemes, even tentatively embracing the tradition of Sunday roasts, Kayode and Amina had begun to bridge the gap. They learned to appreciate the subtle humour, the unspoken social codes, and the underlying sense of community that permeated their neighbourhood. It wasn’t about erasing their cultural identity, but about enriching it, about finding a harmonious balance between their heritage and their new surroundings. They were learning to be not just Nigerians in the UK, but residents, neighbours, and active members of their community, contributing to its vibrancy in their own unique way.

This renegotiation of their reality was not a destination but a continuous journey. There were still moments of uncertainty, days when the weight of expectations felt heavy and nostalgia for home was sharp. But now they faced these challenges not as individuals adrift but as a unified front, their bonds strengthened by shared experience and deepening mutual understanding. Kayode realised the dream hadn't been a static blueprint but a living, evolving entity, shaped and reshaped by the realities of their new life. It now encompassed not just material security and educational opportunities for their children but also a profound sense of belonging, a rich tapestry of shared experiences, and the quiet satisfaction of having built a life, not despite their challenges but because of them. Payoffs, once deferred to a distant future, were now realised in everyday moments. They were in Mayo's confident stride as she left for school, Kofi's bright laughter as he practised with his rock band, family vacations, quiet evenings with Amina planning their next adventure, and the shared pride in the home they had built, brick by brick. This was the unfolding future, a testament to their resilience, adaptability, and the enduring power of a promise, redefined and ultimately fulfilled.

GLIMMERS OF HOPE AND ENDURING CHALLENGES

The initial euphoria of settling, of having navigated the tumultuous currents of immigration and found a semblance of shore, was fragile, like a delicate bloom exposed to an unexpected frost. Kayode and Amina had, indeed, found their footing. The relentless grind was beginning to yield tangible results. Kayode's role at the firm, initially a precarious foothold, had solidified. He was no longer the 'new boy', the one whose every utterance was scrutinised for potential misunderstandings, but a valued member of the team. His meticulous work, innovative problem-solving, and unwavering commitment had not gone unnoticed. Promotions, once a distant aspiration, now felt like a plausible, even imminent, reality.

He had learned to navigate the subtle hierarchies and the unspoken rules of corporate culture, and to leverage his unique perspective, honed by years of experience in a different professional landscape, to his advantage. The satisfaction that came with this professional recognition was a powerful balm, a validation of the sacrifices made. It wasn't just about the salary increase, though that was undeniably crucial, but about the feeling of contributing, of being seen and appreciated for his skills and intellect. He found quiet pride in mentoring younger colleagues, sharing his knowledge, and seeing them grow, a reflection of his own journey.

Amina's venture into catering, which had begun as a small, hesitant side hustle, had blossomed into a genuine enterprise. The aroma of her meticulously prepared dishes, a fragrant echo of home, had begun to fill the kitchens of discerning clients across the city.

She had started with small gatherings, friends and acquaintances captivated by her authentic flavours and impeccable service. Word of mouth, the most potent of endorsements, had spread like wildfire. Soon, she was catering for corporate events, weddings, and significant family celebrations. The late nights spent chopping, marinating, and perfecting recipes were still a reality. Yet they were infused with a different kind of energy – the thrill of creation, the joy of bringing pleasure to others through her culinary artistry. She had found her niche, a space where her passion and her heritage could converge, creating something unique and deeply fulfilling. The pride she felt when a client raved about her signature jollof rice or her delicate chin chin was immeasurable. She had transformed a beloved hobby into a thriving business, demonstrating a tenacity and entrepreneurial spirit that had surprised even herself.

The children, too, were no longer the hesitant newcomers they had once been. Kofi, now comfortably ensconced in the rhythm of secondary school, had found his tribe. His initial shyness had given way to confident engagement with his studies and a burgeoning passion for music. His accent was now a charming blend of his heritage and his adopted home. He had discovered a talent for performance and a natural flair for storytelling that had surprised his parents, who had always seen him as the more introspective of their two children. He was not only excelling academically but also actively participating in school concerts, his stage presence captivating.

Maya, ever the social butterfly, had seamlessly integrated into her senior high school. Her infectious laughter and bright, curious mind had made her a favourite among her peers and teachers alike. She was a regular name on the list of achievers at the school's prize-giving, her days filled with joyful friendships and the excitement of learning new things. They were no longer just surviving; they were thriving, building their own futures within the framework of their new reality.

Yet to suggest that the challenges had entirely dissipated would be to paint a picture as simplistic as the initial dream that had fuelled their 'japa'. The UK, for all its opportunities, remained a land of subtle barriers and persistent complexities. Kayode found himself increasingly aware of the invisible ceilings that sometimes seemed to cap his professional ascent. While his immediate superiors valued his contributions, he sensed a subtle reserve, a hesitance in some quarters to fully embrace a leader from a different cultural background. The 'old boys' network, that often-unspoken fraternity, remained a formidable, albeit invisible, force. He had to work twice as hard, be twice as articulate, and be twice as prepared to command the same level of respect afforded to some of his less experienced, but more 'culturally aligned,' colleagues.

The pressure to assimilate, to conform to a specific unwritten code of conduct, was a constant, low-level hum beneath the surface of his professional interactions. He had learned to adapt, to speak the language of corporate politics. Still, there were moments when the sheer effort of it all felt exhausting, and it felt more like a constant performance than an authentic expression of his capabilities.

Amina, despite the success of her catering business, still grappled with the inherent instability of self-employment. The feast-or-famine nature of her industry meant that periods of intense work were followed by quieter spells, necessitating constant vigilance and proactive marketing. The administrative burdens, endless paperwork, VAT returns, and ever-changing food safety regulations were a constant drain on her time and energy, diverting her from the creative process she loved most. She also found herself navigating a landscape of expectations that differed from what she had anticipated.

While her clients appreciated her culinary skills, there were still instances when her cultural background was portrayed as exotic and her dishes viewed as novelties rather than the sophisticated cuisine they truly were. She longed for the day when her cooking would be appreciated for its intrinsic merit, not merely as a representation of her heritage. Furthermore, the constant need to balance her business demands with her roles as a mother, wife, and pillar of her growing community left her perpetually stretched thin.

The family's dynamics, while strengthened by their shared journey, were also evolving in new and sometimes challenging ways. As Kofi and Maya grew into young adults, their individual aspirations and desires began to diverge.

Maya was showing increasing independence and a keen sense of her own identity, shaped by her Nigerian and British upbringing. She had her own opinions, her own friends, and her own vision of what her future might hold, which sometimes seemed less connected to the cultural traditions that were so important to her parents. Amina found it challenging to reconcile

Maya's emerging sense of self with the cultural values she held dear. There were moments of gentle friction and unspoken disappointment as Maya navigated her teenage years, asserting her individuality in ways that sometimes felt like a rejection of her heritage. These were the quiet battles of diaspora, the subtle shifts in allegiance as the second generation forged its own path, a path that would inevitably diverge, at least in part, from that of their parents. Despite these ongoing challenges, the 'glimmers of hope' were undeniable. The sheer fact of their continued presence, their resilience, and their unwavering commitment to each other was a testament to their strength. They had not just survived; they were building a life, a legacy. Kayode and Amina had found a profound appreciation for the small victories. They had learned to savour these moments, to hold onto them as anchors in the unpredictable seas of immigrant life.

Their commitment to their community had also deepened. They were no longer merely recipients of support; they were active contributors, volunteering their time in their local communities. They understood that their successes were intrinsically linked to the well-being of the wider community, and they were committed to fostering a sense of belonging and mutual support. They had learned that the diaspora, while often isolating, could also be a source of immense collective strength, a shared experience that transcended individual differences.

In their eyes, the UK was no longer merely a destination, a place of promised prosperity, but a complex, evolving landscape they were actively shaping. They were not simply adapting to it; they were contributing to its tapestry, adding their own unique threads of culture, experience, and resilience. The initial dream of 'japa' had been about escape and betterment. But the reality, the unfolding future, was about something far richer and more profound: about building, contributing, and forging a new identity that embraced both their heritage and their adopted home. They knew that new challenges would inevitably arise, that the journey was far from over. There would be further adjustments, further negotiations, further moments of doubt and uncertainty. But they also knew they faced these challenges not as individuals adrift but as a family, bound by a shared history, a common purpose, and an enduring spirit forged in the crucible of their extraordinary journey. The future, though still an unfolding narrative, held not just the promise of more challenges but also the certainty of continued growth, deeper connections, and a life lived with purpose and profound gratitude. The story, they understood, was not in reaching a destination but in the ongoing, dynamic process of living, learning, and loving in this new yet increasingly familiar land.

LESSONS LEARNT IN THE DIASPORA

The dust of arrival had long settled, replaced by the persistent sounds of daily life in this new land. Yet the echoes of the journey, both literal and metaphorical, continued to resonate. It was in these quiet moments, often late at night when the house was still and the weight of the day's efforts settled, that the proper lessons of the diaspora began to crystallise. The initial dream of 'japa', that fervent desire to escape and ascend, had been a potent, all-consuming force. It painted a picture of immediate betterment, unlocked opportunities, and promised a smoother, more prosperous existence. But the reality, as Kayode and Amina had discovered, was as complex as a tapestry woven with threads of sacrifice, unexpected challenges, and profound personal growth. What they came to understand, with a clarity born of experience, was that 'japa' was rarely a simple escape, a clean break from the old to embrace the new. Instead, it was a profound, often brutal, metamorphosis. It demanded not just a physical relocation but an internal seismic shift. The economic pressures, usually the primary driver, were indeed significant, but they were merely one facet of a much higher, more intricate cost.

The emotional toll, for instance, was a relentless undercurrent, a constant negotiation with feelings of displacement, loneliness, and the ache of being separated from the familiar. Amina, who had always found solace in the embrace of her extended family and the comforting rituals of their community, felt the absence keenly. The casual drop-ins, the shared meals, the collective worry and celebration – these were not easily replicated. She had tried to recreate them, inviting neighbours and friends over, but there was an indescribable quality missing, a deep-rooted familiarity that transcended mere social interaction. Kayode, too, grappled with this, finding his usual easy-going nature tested by the sheer effort required to build new social networks from scratch. The old friendship, the shorthand of shared experiences and understanding, was absent, and each new interaction felt deliberate, sometimes exhausting.

The financial reality, while ultimately leading to the stability they sought, was a far more precarious tightrope walk than they had initially envisioned. The cost of living, unexpected fees, and the initial period of settling debts and establishing credit – all of it put an immense strain on their savings. What had seemed a substantial cushion back home felt alarmingly fragile here. During those early months, the sheer weight of their financial obligations felt suffocating. Every purchase, no matter how small, was scrutinised, and every expenditure felt like a risk. This constant economic anxiety seeped into their everyday lives, creating a low-level tension that was difficult to shake. It meant delayed gratification of personal desires, fewer outings, and a constant internal calculus of needs versus wants. This was not the carefree prosperity they had perhaps subconsciously imagined, but a hard-won, meticulously managed stability.

Perhaps one of the most significant, and often overlooked, casualties of this relentless pursuit of a better future was the marital relationship itself. The shared dream of 'japa' had been a powerful unifying force during the planning stages, a beacon of hope that bound Kayode and Amina together. But the immense pressures of establishing a new life, such as, long working hours, financial worries, and the emotional strain of adapting began to create cracks. They were often exhausted, and their communication became utilitarian, focused on logistics and problem-solving rather than the deeper emotional connection that had always sustained them. Arguments, when they arose, felt amplified by stress, and the usual mechanisms of reconciliation such as a shared laugh, a comforting embrace, a mutual understanding born of shared history were far-fetched.

Amina would sometimes catch herself staring at Kayode across the dinner table, a stranger in his weariness, and a clove of sadness would strike her.

Where was the easy joy, the shared laughter that had once been the soundtrack to their lives? It was still there, she knew, buried beneath layers of fatigue and responsibility, but it required a conscious, concerted effort to unearth it. They had to actively work to remember why they had embarked on this journey together, reminding each other of their shared love and mutual commitment, not just to their children's future, but also to their own partnership.

The impact on the children, while ultimately positive in terms of their adaptation and resilience, was also a source of significant parental anxiety. The initial period of adjustment for Maya and Kofi had been a delicate dance. While they were strong, their youthful spirits were not immune to the challenges. Amina had agonised over the moments of sadness or frustration she perceived in them. Had they been too quick to uproot them? Had they traded their children's immediate happiness for a future that still felt abstract? She remembered Kofi's quiet withdrawal in the first few years, his preference for the digital world, and Maya's occasional wistfulness for her friends back home. These were not dramatic outbursts but subtle shifts that spoke volumes about the emotional undercurrents of their transition. The parents had to learn to read these cues, offer reassurance without undermining the reality of their situation, and celebrate every small victory, every new friendship formed, and every moment of laughter and connection.

They had to trust in their children's inborn resilience, a trust constantly tested by the unknown complexities of their developing lives.

This journey had underscored the paramount importance of realistic expectations. The glossy brochures and aspirational stories often painted an incomplete picture, omitting the grit, compromise, and sheer tenacity required. Kayode and Amina, perhaps, had been guilty of a certain naivety, fuelled by an eagerness for a better life. They had envisioned a smoother ascent, a more linear progression. They now understood that adaptation was not a single event but an ongoing process, a continuous series of adjustments and recalibrations. Each new phase of life in the UK brought its own set of challenges, from navigating the complexities of the education system to understanding the nuances of the job market and social etiquette. They learned that the promise of a better future was not a static destination but a dynamic horizon that shifted and evolved as they moved towards it.

Communication within the family had become not just a tool for planning but a lifeline. They had learned to talk, honestly, about their fears, frustrations, and hopes. Kayode, who tended to internalise his worries, had to learn to voice them, to share the burden with Amina. Amina, in turn, had to be more attuned to Kayode's unspoken anxieties and express her own needs more clearly. They instituted regular "family check-ins," not formal meetings but informal moments where each person had space to share how they were feeling. These check-ins opened avenues for understanding, empathy, and collective problem-solving. When Maya struggled with a particular aspect of her schoolwork, or when

Kofi felt overwhelmed by a social situation, these open lines of communication allowed Kayode and Amina to offer targeted support, rather than guesswork. They learned that the strength of their family unit was directly proportional to the honesty and depth of their interactions.

The diaspora had, in essence, stripped away many of the superficial comforts and familiar structures of their previous life, forcing them to confront themselves and each other more fundamentally. The lessons learned were not abstract philosophical pronouncements but intuitive, lived experiences. They had learned that true strength lay not in the absence of hardship but in the capacity to navigate it with grace and resilience. They had learned that the most valuable assets were not material possessions but the bonds of family, the unwavering spirit of perseverance, and the profound understanding that came with every obstacle they overcame.

The 'japa' journey had been arduous, marked by unforeseen costs and demanding sacrifices. Still, in its wake, it had forged a family unit that was not just surviving but truly thriving, grounded in a hard-won wisdom that promised to see them through whatever future lay ahead. They had arrived seeking a promise, and as their lives unfolded, they discovered a richer, more profound payoff: the enduring strength of their collective spirit.

RESOURCES

The themes and experiences in this book have come from the experiences of many migrates and were obtained through interviews, community dialogue, observations, research and friendly chats. In addition, the listed works below have helped to provide invaluable context and understanding of the experiences of immigrants in the UK:

Adepoju, A. (2017). *The African Diaspora in Europe: A Comparative Analysis*. While not a single published book, Adepoju's extensive research and publications with organisations such as the UN Population Division have been foundational in understanding migration patterns and the challenges faced by African migrants in Europe.

Gilroy, P. (2000). *Between Melancholy and Xenophobia: Black British Identity in the Age of Fortress Europe*. This influential work explores the complexities of Black British identity and the socio-political climate impacting minority communities in the UK.

Modood, T. (2005). *Multiculturalism: A Civic Idea*. Modood's exploration of multiculturalism offers critical insights into debates over integration, identity, and citizenship for ethnic minorities in contemporary Britain.

Phillips, A. (2006). *The Politics of the English Language*. Phillips' work offers a compelling examination of how language is used to construct and maintain social hierarchies, particularly relevant to understanding subtle forms of exclusion.

Research on the economic and social impacts of immigration in the UK, particularly reports on institutions such as the Migration Observatory at the University of Oxford and the Centre for Economic Performance at the London School of Economics.

Statistics and trends regarding employment, entrepreneurship, and social integration are also reflected in the characters' experiences.

www.ingramcontent.com/pod-product-compliance
Lightning Source LLC
LaVergne TN
LVHW091128080826
845145LV00008B/2083

* 9 7 8 1 0 3 6 9 5 0 0 7 1 *